Collectors' Information Bureau's

DIRECTORY TO SECONDARY MARKET RETAILERS

Buying and Selling Limited Edition Artwork

Diane Carnevale Jones

Collectors' Information Bureau
2420 Burton S.E.
Grand Rapids, Michigan 49546
(616) 942-6898

Acknowledgments

The premier issue of any book requires extra time and effort from all parties involved. The Collectors' Information Bureau extends its deep gratitude to the participants of this book. May these dedicated and enthusiastic individuals gain many new customers and friends, as they educate collectors about the secondary market.

The Collectors' Information Bureau would like to thank the following persons who have contributed to the creation of this book: Dan Nichols, Wm. C. Brown & Co.; and Linda L. Joswick, Laurie Schaut, Dave Stafford and Joy Versluys, all with Trade Typographers, Inc.

Teamwork is the key to any successful project. The executive director wishes to thank her staff who contributed countless hours to the creation of this book: Sue Knappen, who worked with the directory participants on their editorial material; Carol Van Elderen, who worked with the participants and at the computer; Cindy Zagumny, our expert proofreader; and college interns, Emily Eldersveld and Bethany Kuiper, who had their first taste of publishing and deadlines!

A special thank you is also extended to the Collectors' Information Bureau's Board of Directors who were very supportive of this new venture: Heio W. Reich, Reco International; James P. Smith, Jr., The Hamilton Collection; Ronald Jedlinski, Roman, Inc.; Bruce Kollath, John Hine Studios, Inc.; John Conley, Enesco Corporation; and Susan K. Jones, special consultant.

CREDITS:

Book Design and Graphics: Laurie Schaut, Trade Typographers, Inc., Grand Rapids, Michigan

Contents

A Warm Welcome from The Collectors' Information Bureau

by Diane Carnevale Jones
Executive Director

In 1982, 14 collectible manufacturers became charter members of the Collectors' Information Bureau (CIB), which was formed to increase the public's awareness of the collectibles industry, an industry which has experienced extraordinary growth and collector enthusiasm in recent years. Today, the Collectors' Information Bureau is recognized as an authoritative source within the industry, providing the most accurate and up-to-date information on limited edition plates, figurines, bells, graphics, ornaments, dolls and steins. Entering its tenth year, this not-for-profit organization has nearly 70 member companies and reaches out to thousands of collectors across the country and around the world!

Books! Books! Books!

Collectors who enjoy reading about their hobby will enjoy the variety of books published by the Collectors' Information Bureau.

The *Collectibles Market Guide & Price Index* offers collectors nearly 500 pages of comprehensive information about most every aspect of collecting. Illustrated feature articles, a secondary market Price Index, manufacturer profiles, artist biographies and a complete listing of collector clubs are among the many topics covered in this ever-expanding edition. Rich color abounds on the cover and within the book, making this annual guide a 'must' for every collector.

The *Collectibles Price Guide*, published mid-year, features a Price Index listing over 25,000 active market prices based upon constant communication with a panel of expert retailers throughout North America, who buy and sell retired collectibles. Collectors who insure their artwork against theft and breakage, find this price guide an invaluable document, as well as hobbyists who buy and sell retired collectibles on the secondary market.

The Collectors' Information Bureau headquarters receives hundreds of phone calls from collectors who are interested in participating in the secondary market, yet need more information about the mechanics behind this venture. In an effort to educate collectors about this area, the Bureau makes available this, the premiere edition of *Directory to Secondary Market Retailers: Buying and Selling Limited Edition Artwork*. This book features a comprehensive listing of today's most respected secondary market dealers and exchanges nationwide, in addition to a practical guide outlining the basics of secondary market trading.

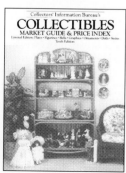

The Collectibles Market Guide & Price Index

Collectibles Price Guide

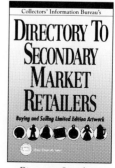

Directory to Secondary Market Retailers

Operation "Collector Hotline"

The Collectors' Information Bureau offers a hotline number to assist collectors with their difficult-to-answer questions. By calling (616) 942-9'CIB', collectors receive personal assistance in locating information on their favorite artists, phone numbers of manufacturers or perhaps values for their collectibles. Any questions that cannot be answered by phone are then directed to the research staff, who mail responses to collectors, once the information has been located.

COLLECTIBLES HOTLINE
CALL (616) 942-9 "CIB"

THE SOURCE FOR LIMITED EDITION COLLECTIBLE INFORMATION:

Plates, Figurines, Bells, Graphics, Christmas Ornaments, Dolls, Steins

Collectors' Information Bureau, 2420 Burton S.E.
Grand Rapids, MI 49546, Fax (616) 942-8594

Media Blitz

The Collectors' Information Bureau is actively involved in the media, both in supplying collectibles information to the top 500 daily newspapers, in addition to writing several magazine columns for collectible publications. Executive Director Diane Carnevale Jones has also appeared on cable television and has participated in numerous radio talk shows on the subject of collecting.

Newsletters, Collector Conventions and Seminars

The "C.I.B. Report" newsletter, published three times annually, contains the latest collectibles news, including recent product introductions, collector club activities, artist open houses, product retirement announcements and convention news. These 32-page color newsletters are distributed at national collector conventions, through retailers and directly to collectors who purchase CIB books.

The Collectors' Information Bureau's booth at the International Collectible Exposition was staffed by (L to R) Diane Carnevale Jones, Sue Knappen and Cindy Zagumny. This show, held each July in South Bend, Indiana and one other collector show held in the Spring on either the East or West Coast, is managed by McRand International, Ltd. of Lake Forest, Illinois.

The Collectors' Information Bureau, along with scores of manufacturers, exhibit at annual national collector conventions on the east and west coasts, as well as in South Bend, Indiana. Thousands of collectors attend these events, strolling through exhibition halls viewing recent product introductions, meeting the artists who create these products and attending seminars. The Collectors' Information Bureau is on hand to distribute newsletters, answer collectors' secondary market questions and to present seminars on this same topic.

The Collectors' Information Bureau looks to new opportunities and challenges as the organization continues to expand its services, offering accurate, up-to-date and educational information to collectors, retailers, manufacturers and the media. We remain "**the** source for limited edition collectibles information!"

The Secondary Market

Leading Dealers Share Their Hard-Won Knowledge About Buying and Selling Collectibles on the Secondary Market

by Diane Carnevale Jones and Susan K. Jones

Department 56's "Original Shops of Dickens' Village" issued for $175 in 1984, and the set is now valued at $1100-$1800 in mint condition. Gartlan USA's personally signed "Joe DiMaggio" figurine was introduced for $275 in 1989 and is currently listed at $850-$1000. Flambro Imports' Emmett Kelly, Jr. "Looking Out to See" figurine was released in 1981 at $75, and the retired figurine is now selling for $1500-$3200.

The idea of placing a value on a piece of artwork or purchasing a limited edition collectible for investment purposes is a subject many collectors are eager to study—the secondary market.

We recently overheard a well-known collectibles producer bemoaning the fact that one of his loveliest plates would never see significant secondary market action. "We introduced it in a limited edition of just 1,000," the gentleman explained, "and so few people have ever heard of it or seen it that it has never penetrated the market!"

Imagine that: a limited edition collectible whose edition is too small to ensure its opportunity for secondary market price rises! Novices in the field would be sure to surmise just the opposite: aren't we all taught from childhood that the rarer an item is, the more likely it is to appreciate in value?

The fact is that in today's international collectibles market, with millions of enthusiastic art lovers vying to own the most popular works, a piece with a relatively large edition may well "outperform" an extremely limited plate, figurine or other collectible. Why? Because the key to the market is supply and demand.

If available supply is less than pent-up demand for a given work of art, that piece's price most often will begin to climb on the auction market. Demand cannot be stimulated without collectors' knowledge of the item's existence. And those items which are seen throughout the marketplace are most likely to attract and sustain the interest of a broad range of collectors.

This short "object lesson" is meant to illustrate a point. Today's market for limited edition collectibles is complex, exciting and fast-paced. And its patterns of success do not necessarily "square" with a collector's experience in financial markets or other aspects of life.

There is a great deal to learn and understand in order to make the best buying and selling decisions. And to gather this valuable knowledge for our readers, Collectors' Information Bureau has interviewed more than 20 top limited edition dealers who are actively involved in today's secondary market for plates, figurines, bells, graphics, ornaments and dolls.

What Is the Secondary Market?

To begin, let us establish the step-by-step process by which a limited edition collectible enters the secondary market.

1. A collectible is introduced to the market and made available to collectors. Collectors may purchase the item through a dealer (in person or by mail or phone), or direct from the manufacturer/marketer (usually by mail or phone only). Items are sold at "original issue price," which is their retail price level. This method of selling is known as the "primary market."

2. After a period which may vary from days to years, the collectible becomes "sold out." This means that neither the dealers nor the manufacturer/marketers have any additional pieces to sell to collectors on the primary market.

3. When a collector wishes to buy a piece which is "sold out," he or she must enter the "secondary market" to purchase it. Because the piece is no longer available at retail, the new buyer must locate someone who already owns it and pay whatever price the market will bear. Most buyers enlist the help of a dealer, exchange or matching service to help

them in this process, while some place want ads in collectibles publications, or "network" with fellow collectors.

4. If new buyers continue to seek to acquire the piece long after its edition is sold out, the secondary market for that item may become stronger and stronger, and the price it can command may multiply over and over. Such market action is reported in price guides as located for example, in the Collectors' Information Bureau books.

Of course, some collectibles never sell out completely, while others sell out but never attract sufficient demand to command a higher price than the issue-price level. Some collectibles peak soon after their editions close, while others remain dormant for years and then begin rising in value because of changing market dynamics.

Manufacturers, dealers and collectible experts alike caution all collectors to *buy items that they like and want to display*, without regard for possible price rises. No one knows for certain whether a given item will end up rising in value on the secondary market.

How Collectible Editions are Limited

The term "limited edition" is one that many collectors find confusing, since studios limit production of their collectibles in many different ways. Here is an explanation of the most common methods of edition limitation.

Limited by Number: The producer sets a worldwide edition limit which may be a round number, or a number with special significance. Gartlan USA, for example, often limits its sports collectibles to numbers that have importance in the careers of the sports celebrities they depict. Such items may carry their own sequential numbers within the edition.

Limited by Time: The producer pledges to craft an item only during a specific time period: the year 1992, for instance. A Christmas plate might close its edition on Christmas Eve of the year of issue, as another example. Or a commemorative figurine might be offered for the two years prior to a historic event, then close its edition on the date of the event. Such items may carry their own sequential numbers within the edition.

Limited by Firing Period: This designation has to do with the number of items that can be kiln-fired by a marketer or producer in a given number of days. It is stated in terms such as "limited to a total of 14 firing days." Items limited by firing period most often are sequentially numbered on the backstamp or bottomstamp.

Limited to Members: In recent years, many collectors clubs have offered "members-only" items that are available only during a set time period, and only to individuals who have joined the club. A secondary market for these items develop when individuals join the club in later years and wish to acquire earlier editions of "members-only" collectibles that are no longer available at retail.

Open Editions that are Closed or Retired: While open editions are not strictly considered limited editions, they may stimulate secondary market action when they are closed or retired, and are no longer available at original-issue price.

Advice to Collectors Entering the Secondary Market

In recent years, the secondary market has become more sophisticated. Collectors are becoming more knowledgeable about their hobby and the secondary market and making their purchases based upon this information. In a survey conducted by the Collectors' Information Bureau, however, only 20% of collectors have bought or sold collectibles on the secondary market. Even for those who have traded on the secondary market, most admit that buying for investment is *not* their primary reason for collecting.

Deciding how to go about buying and selling on the secondary market, and what "philosophy of collecting" to adopt can be challenging to collectors. Here, some words of wisdom from experienced dealers provide guidelines to new and seasoned collectors.

When considering the sale of an item, the first step is to "determine the present secondary market value of the collectible," according to Lynda Blankenship of Dickens' Exchange in Metairie, Louisiana. Ms. Blankenship advises collectors to check the latest Price Guide from Collectors' Information Bureau or monthly update reports in collectibles magazines for prices. "Or contact a secondary market broker for an opinion," she suggests.

Being realistic in setting a price is important, says Bob Phillips of The Wishing Well in Solvang, California. "Don't think that your piece is worth more than the other person's or you'll be hanging onto it longer than you want," Phillips cautions. Sandie Ellis of Ellis in Wonderland, Sacramento, California, echoes his advice and adds a comment of her own. "If you are looking for a quick sale, set the price below market; otherwise be prepared to wait," she says.

Sometimes a buyer is waiting in the wings in your own "backyard," according to Reda Walsh of The Kent Collection in Englewood, Colorado. That's why Ms. Walsh advises collectors to "check with your local retail dealer first to see if they are looking" for the items you have to sell. Another possibility, according to Marge Rosenberg of Carol's Gift Shop, Artesia California, is selling through a local collectors club. "Most of them have Swap and Sell events at their meetings," she explains.

In setting prices, collectors should understand that the amount they clear from the sale of an item will depend upon how they arrange to sell it. The prices quoted in most price guides—including the Collectors' Information Bureau's—are retail prices. Any brokerage fees, commissions, consignment fees or cost of ads will be deducted from this price. What's more, price quotes represent an average or price range: an item may command more at certain times and in certain areas of the country and less in others depending upon supply and demand.

In addition, price quotes assume that the item is perfect—in mint condition. Chips, repairs, discolorations, production flaws, damage or other imperfections will negatively impact the selling price in most cases. As the seller, you should be straightforward about your collectible's condition, says Patricia Cantrell of Village Realty Miniature Properties, Fort Worth, Texas. "If any problems are found, they should be noted and the prospective buyer made aware of them," she cautions.

Sandy Forgach of Collectibles, etc., Inc. Match Service and Gift Shop says that cleaning one's collectibles before selling them will help maximize the price they can command. "People often make no effort to clean them," Ms. Forgach says, but a dusty and dingy piece is much less likely to bring a top price than one which is mint-condition clean.

Making Smooth Buying Transactions on the Secondary Market

In addition to the often-heard advice to "buy only what you like," experienced dealers have much to share in the way of guidelines for secondary market buyers. Their most frequent comment is to be sure that you know whom you are dealing with: the choice of a broker, buy-sell service or other "go-between" is often even more important for the buyer than it is for the seller.

Sandy Forgach suggests paying with a charge card when you buy from an ad. This offers you protection in case the item is not in mint condition or does not arrive as promised. "When you pay by check, you assume all the risks," she explains.

Connie Eckman of Collectible Exchange Inc. in New Middletown, Ohio, advises collectors to buy only the items they need to fill in collections they're working on. She has found that people who purchase an item only in the hopes that it will rise in value—so they can sell at a profit—are often disappointed. "Speculating at secondary prices rarely pays off," she says.

"Don't just shop in your own backyard," says Lynda Blankenship. Take advantage of possible regional differences in price by checking around. "If a piece is constantly available at the same price, it is obviously not a fabulous deal," Ms. Blankenship continues. Education, patience and staying abreast of the market will yield the best possible bargain, she believes.

Those who plan on buying via the secondary market should "go on mailing lists of as many reputable secondary market dealers as possible," says Becky Flynn of Dollsville Dolls and Bearsville Bears in Palm Springs, California. This will enable the collector to research items just by reading over the mail they receive. While there is some controversy over the necessity of obtaining boxes, certificates and other materials that originally accompanied the collectible, it is in the buyer's best interest to receive this material if at all possible. In this case, an experienced and reputable dealer or broker can be of help in determining what came with the collectible upon its arrival from the producer. "Be certain all necessary papers, Certificates of Authenticity, etc. are available at the time of purchase," says Karen Wilson of Callahan's of Calabash Nautical Gifts, Calabash, North Carolina.

Finally, a collector should rationally assess what a piece is worth to him or her and make buying decisions accordingly. In the heat of an auction situation, collectors may bid a piece up to 20 or 30 times its original price and still be happy to get it. Other collectors are more conservative, perhaps to their later regret. As Renee Tyler of Collector's Marketplace in Montrose, Pennsylvania says, "I've seen people miss a great chance to get something special because of a $25.00 difference in price."

The C.I.B. Price Index Offers a Starting Point for Secondary Prices

Collectors are also encouraged to study the market and become knowledgeable about every aspect of the field. Price guides are particularly helpful to collectors who are inclined to purchase art as an investment or for those individuals who find themselves in a position to sell their collection. The Collectors' Information Bureau publishes one of the most comprehensive price indices in the marketplace today, covering the market for limited edition plates, figurines, bells, dolls, graphics, ornaments and steins.

As with any price index, a collector must look upon secondary market information as a guide and not the value of an item right down to the penny. Some collectibles retain the same relative value for years, while others rise and fall faster than the information is printed.

The Collectors' Information Bureau Price Index is prepared very carefully. Manufacturers supply all pertinent product information to the Bureau. This data is then entered into a computer, and copies of the Price Index are then mailed to experts nationwide. These qualified dealers and exchanges report actual sales transactions, whose values may vary throughout the country. Therefore, a price or price range is determined for each entry, based upon careful analysis of the reports. Over 25,000 values are entered in the Collectors' Information Bureau's Price Index, which is then published annually in the fall and updated in the spring.

Specific Ways to Buy and Sell Collectibles

Collectors who wish to—or need to—sell their treasured collectibles, may consider several methods of doing so. Here are details on each procedure:

Place a Classified Ad. Advertising in publications such as *The Antique Trader, Collectors News* and *Doll Reader*, offer collectors the opportunity to work without 'third party' involvement, thereby eliminating the commission paid to a middle man. The cost of an ad is minimal, but collectors should have some knowledge of how to complete transactions by mail. Most publications offer guidelines to their advertisers to assist them in trading through the mail.

Retail Dealers. Collectible retailers may also assist collectors by acting as a broker for a sales transaction. The fact is that very few retailers participate in the secondary market. Some feel that a collector should buy what they like and enjoy the artwork. Others have no understanding of the secondary market or don't keep up with the latest quotes and in fact, may have no interest in this area.

There are, however, retailers who are fascinated with the secondary market, who find the sales very profitable and are willing to help collectors sell their artwork. Where do collectors locate these retailers? They can look in publications such as *The Antique Trader, Collector Editions, Dolls* and *Collectors News*, where dealers advertise regularly. In addition, *The Directory to Secondary Market Retailers* features dozens of dealers and exchanges who can assist collectors in their quest for retired artwork.

Retailers handle their secondary market transactions in several ways. They may accept items on consignment and consequently reimburse the collector for their limited edition, once it has been sold. Many dealers use a filing system or computer and the telephone to match up buyers and sellers. And others may make an outright purchase of collectibles which have exhibited significant secondary market increases. In any case, a commission or brokerage fee is charged to the seller. It is very important to inquire about this fee IN ADVANCE, because fees vary dramatically—anywhere between 5% and 50%.

Buy/Sell Exchanges. Collector exchanges began popping up across the country a few years ago, making secondary market trading more accessible for thousands of collectors. Many have 800 numbers, and all charge a commission or brokerage fee to the seller and sometimes the buyer. Once again, it is wise to ask for information before deciding which firm to employ. Exchanges are not active on the primary market. Rather, they are in the business of matching up buyers and sellers and offering each party certain guarantees. The buyer is guaranteed the retired piece he is purchasing is in mint condition. The seller is guaranteed prompt and proper payment for the collectible, once the transaction has been completed. Each exchange operates differently. Some will charge a membership or listing fee, while others have no fees other than the sales commission. Chuck Eckman from the Collectible Exchange, Inc. out of New Middleton, Ohio explains his firm's procedure. Collectors are invited to call the company's 800 number to list their collectibles on the exchange, supplying an asking price. Once an interested buyer is located, the buyer sends a check to the exchange and the seller mails the piece to be examined by Chuck and his staff before it is forwarded to the buyer. Once the check has cleared, and the piece has been examined by the prospective buyer and approved, the transaction is completed, with the seller receiving his check, minus the commission.

Swap Meets and Auctions. Collectibles may also be sold at swap meets and auctions. Thousands of collectors gather at conventions each year to view manufacturers' booths and learn more about the newest collectibles. Conventions usually feature a 'swap and sell,' where collectors can rent tables for a modest fee. Once again, this is an opportunity for collectors to sell directly to other collectors, thereby avoiding a commission. Local collector clubs and retailers across the United

States also offer swap meets and auctions as a regular part of their activities. Many of these gatherings are advertised in collectibles publications.

Collector shows are popping up all across the country, arranged by show promoters (refer to Eve's Collectors' Show in this book for a description of this type of show). Some shows are geared toward one type of collectible such as Christmas ornaments, while others include collectibles of all kinds. Secondary market dealers and other firms rent table space at these shows and sell retired collectibles to the public. Some shows include seminars, manufacturers reps and drawings to liven these get-togethers.

Secondary Market
Action is Sought by Only a Few

Our dealer experts agree that the vast majority of collectors purchase their items with very little thought of secondary market potential. At the most, they look forward to showing off their "smart buys" to friends as they watch prices rise for their favorite collectibles.

Most secondary market buys, our experts say, are executed by collectors who are hoping to fill out a series or acquire an item of special significance that they were unable to purchase on the primary market.

Some sellers enjoy "trading up" to more expensive collectibles, and finance their new purchases by selling items that once were quite affordable—but now command high prices on the auction market. There are also a number of collectors who wish to sell certain items because of a lifestyle change, a move to smaller quarters, or financial hardship. And sometimes those who inherit collections are not in a position to keep and display them.

Whatever a collector's reason for buying or selling on the secondary market, the keys to success are education, patience, rational thinking and advice from the experts. That includes ready access to the resources of Collectors' Information Bureau. For answers to your secondary market questions, send a self-addressed, stamped envelope to the Collectors' Information Bureau at 2420 Burton S.E., Grand Rapids, Michigan 49546.

Questions—and Answers!
—on Secondary Market Procedures
by Diane Carnevale Jones

Q: How do you determine when to sell collectibles on the secondary market?

A: I always tell collectors that if I knew the answer to this question, that I would be living in a luxurious condo in Florida soaking up the sun! You truly never know the *correct* time to buy or sell a collectible, once it has been retired. Once you've made up your mind, never look back and play the 'what if' game. For every time you make the right decision, there is probably another time that you could have bought or sold higher or lower.

Q: Once I decide to sell my collectibles, how shall I proceed?

A: If you own several collectibles, type an inventory of each item, including manufacturer, series, title, issue price, year of issue and artist. A secondary market value should be placed on each item, *before* you list your collectibles. A wise collector is an informed collector who won't be disappointed with the end result.

Q: How long will it take to buy or sell collectibles on the secondary market?

A: A lot longer that most people think! It is important to remember that for every seller, a buyer must be located. Timing is also important, in that sometimes an item needed is not readily available, or just the opposite: the one for sale is not in great demand! Some collectors can wait up to two years to locate a hard-to-find piece. There is a waiting period even for readily available items. Several weeks can elapse by the time buyers and sellers are contacted, collectibles are examined for authenticity and mint condition, checks are run through banks, and pieces are examined by potential buyers. Always check with the firm you are working with to get an idea of the procedure utilized to conduct buy-sell transactions.

Q: Should I buy duplicates of items I think may go up on the secondary market?

A: Experts suggest that first and foremost, collectors should buy what they like. If a collector follows this advice and a collectible does not rise in value, he owns a beautiful piece of artwork that he likes. Very few retailers will encourage collectors to buy duplicates for investment purposes. Collectors are likely to be disappointed if they have guessed incorrectly.

Q: Where do I locate secondary market values?

A: There are many excellent secondary market resources. *Make certain that your source keeps its pricing current.* There is nothing more disappointing than utilizing an old price guide to determine a value and selling price. The Collectors' Information Bureau publishes the most comprehensive and current price index for modern day limited edition plates, figurines (including cottages and crystal), bells, dolls, graphics, Christmas ornaments and steins. The index is published twice annually. There are other price guides on the market, many featuring a single company. However due to the cost of production, these price guides are limited to those companies whose collectibles show marked price increases during the year. Contact the Collectors' Information Bureau for other price guides available or try the public library.

Q: How shall I use price guides when buying and selling collectibles?

A: A price guide is only that—a guide to determine the approximate worth of an item. Some prices go up and down faster than a guide can be printed! Always use your good sense when reading a price guide. If you feel a price is outdated, check another guide or contact the Collectors' Information Bureau for other sources. Always remember that prices quoted in a price guide are for items in mint condition.

Q: What does the term 'mint condition' mean?

A: It can mean many things, depending upon the collectible. In all cases, the term, 'mint,' means not broken. For Christmas ornaments, the term means 'with the box.' The item cannot be chipped or faded by the sun. According to the glossary in the *Collectors' Information Bureau's Collectibles Market Guide & Price Index*, mint means 'a term originally related to the coin collecting hobby; this means that a limited edition item is still in its original, like-new condition, with all accompanying documents.' The documents aforementioned include the Certificate of Authenticity and all other tags that originally accompanied the collectible.

Q: Does the original box make a difference in the secondary market sale of a collectible?

A: Read the following comments from retailers and exchanges across the country and be the judge of this very controversial 'box vs no box' theory:

Collectible Exchange, Inc. (New Middletown, OH): "Most collectors want the original box. Pieces without boxes normally sell at 10-20% less."

Dickens' Exchange (Metairie, LA): "Boxes are extremely valuable and their presence or absence does affect the value on the secondary market. One must remember that a piece will sell on the secondary market without a box, but always for approximately 10% less. The question is always asked: If I purchase this piece without a box, what will happen if I want to sell it later? Always remember that the same rule would apply. If you purchased it at a 10% discount, chances are you will sell it with a 10% discount at the time of sale."

Ellis in Wonderland (Sacramento, CA): "If you have two identical collectibles—one with the box and one without—the collector will always opt for the one with the box."

Collectibles etc., Inc. (Brown Deer, WI): "Except for some older items, most of our items are matched with the box. We have found that boxes do not matter to most people...they just want the item and find storage a 'pain.' People who do save boxes have had to come up with 'creative' ways to store them. There are pros and cons for boxes. They are really handy when shipping to sell or when moving. Our Match Service finds it safer and convenient to have the boxes, but we do not insist. If the customer requires a box, we locate one. Satisfaction is guaranteed!"

The Kent Collection (Englewood, CO): "Boxes ARE important—for storage—for shipping—for giftwrapping—and one never knows which collector is going to insist upon original 'everything.' So we start with 'everything.'"

Collector's Marketplace (Montrose, PA): "All original packaging is important. This includes tags, brochures, etc. The more complete the unit, the more the value."

Miller's Gift Gallery (Eaton, OH): "We do not feel that any packaging should come to play in the value of a collectible on the secondary market. The intrinsic value of a collectible item is in the figurine or material itself inclusive of its workmanship and artistry. The packaging is merely an effective means of transportation for the collectible."

Village Realty Miniature Properties (Fort Worth, TX): "Very important!! Not only do the pieces suffer a 15-20% devaluation...they are very hard to sell without the original boxes to today's sophisticated collectors! Collectors are buying with an eye toward investment value. They not only look for boxes, but for excellent examples in the pieces themselves."

Q: Where should I look for help in buying or selling on the secondary market?

A: When collectors decide to buy or sell retired collectibles, they are often surprised to find they cannot return to the store from which they purchased their items. In fact, there are very few secondary market sources, in comparison to the tens of thousands of collectible gift stores located across the country. Collectors may also experience great difficulty in locating a source that specializes in a particular line of retired items. The Collectors' Information Bureau decided to compile a comprehensive listing of secondary market sources to assist collectors in their quest for retired collectibles. These sources include retailers, exchanges, publications and show promoters. Located in this book are unlimited contacts for plates, figurines, dolls, Christmas ornaments, bells, steins and graphics! Look up your favorite artist or company in the index and find one or more secondary market sources to contact for details.

Q: Secondary market sources use different methods for transacting business. What do all of the terms mean?

A: The following are various terms used as descriptions by directory participants:

Buy outright: Firm will make a cash offer for the retired items. Typically, this offer is far less than the value in a price guide, because cash is offered up front, with no waiting on the collector's end. The business then accepts the merchandise as inventory and sells it as collectors contact them with their requests.

Buy/sell (exchange or brokerage): Buyers and sellers contact these businesses with their secondary market requests. The firm then matches buyers and sellers, usually, but not always, taking a commission from the seller. The firm takes on the liability during the entire exchange — making certain the piece in question is in mint condition — and making sure that the money is collected.

Consignment: A business accepts items from the collector and displays them or advertises them. The seller is then paid a commission, once the item is sold.

Locator service: This term usually refers to a business which specializes in doing research for a buyer looking for a retired collectible. This business normally does not do as much buying of collectibles, but only buys as needed.

Trade: Many collectors want to upgrade their collections by trading in the artwork they already own, for artwork they would prefer to own. Businesses may offer a com-

bination of cash and merchandise for a retired item or offer a straight trade — merchandise, retired or primary — traded for the collector's pieces. Collectors should consider the trade carefully, making certain they are receiving an equitable trade. In many cases, collectors can quickly dispose of items they no longer want, for items (and cash) they prefer to own. Everyone can gain in this situation.

Q: How much should I expect to pay for selling my collectibles?

A: Commissions vary dramatically! In most cases, the seller ends up paying a commission on the item he sells. One of the only ways to avoid a 'third party' commission is to place an ad in a national collectibles publication. The cost of the ad is minimal and may bring successful results. Call the Collectors' Information Bureau for publications that accept secondary market advertisements. Many collectors question what they feel are exhorbitant commissions charged by 'third party' sources. However, if one takes into consideration the time, phone calls and research involved in a typical transaction, in addition to office space and other overhead, the commission does not appear as costly as initially indicated. Commissions vary from 5-50% for the most part. Collectors are encouraged to contact various sources until they have located a business with whom they feel comfortable working.

Q: How easy is it to sell large collections?

A: Selling large collections is very difficult! There are very few businesses who can afford to buy entire collections outright. Don't be surprised when a company offers you a fraction of their worth, when they are offering to buy outright for cash. There are some firms that will take collections on consignment (you give them the collection, and they pay you as the items are sold, minus a commission). Obviously, this method could take months to dispose of an entire collection.

Q: How do I know that I can trust these secondary market experts?

A: The Collectors' Information Bureau does not buy or sell collectibles on the secondary market. Therefore we have no way of guaranteeing a buy-sell transaction. Collectors must take full responsibility for researching their options, as they would in any business transaction. Be sure to ask for references!

Other Helpful Information to Read before Using This Directory:
- **Business hours** are listed according to various time zones. Please use a telephone book or other source before contacting the directory participants.
- **Payment methods** for most firms listed in this directory include check, money order, and charge cards. Please check each business for their terms before conducting business with them.
- **Questions?:** Contact the Collectors' Information Bureau at (616) 942-9242!

Collectors' Information Bureau's

DIRECTORY TO SECONDARY MARKET RETAILERS

Buying and Selling Limited Edition Artwork

Alisa's Dolls

Ramapo Circle
#3 Arapaho Court
Suffern, NY 10901
Phone: 914/368-2509

Alisa's Dolls
specialized in discontinued
& hard to find
limited edition dolls

- **Hours:** Monday-Saturday: 9:00-7:00.

- **Secondary Market Lines:** Lynn and Michael Roche, Annette Himstedt, Yolanda Bello, Turner, Georgetown, Collectables, Dolls by Jerri, Gorham, Patricia Rose, Pat Thompson, Paul Cree, Groessle-Schmidt, Sabine Esche, and one-of-a-kind dolls by Ron Booker, Tom Francerick from First Impressions, Vicki Gunnell, Kristi Hall and many more.

- **Secondary Market Terms:** Doll search. Does not buy outright. Up to five month layaway. Small deposit on dolls ordered. Satisfaction absolutely guaranteed. Will sell to dealers.

- **Business History:** Alisa's Dolls is strictly a mail order business, started by doll collector turned businesswoman, Alisa Benaresh. Alisa, a doll collector herself for over 23 years, began her business in 1988. She is considered a secondary market doll expert in both the contemporary doll market and older dolls.

  Alisa offers extensive individualized attention to her customers, whether they are novice or experienced collectors. She will spend considerable time educating a new collector, or working with an advanced collector who may want to know more about one-of-a-kind dolls or information on investment dolls. Collectors are invited to send for photos, featuring the one-of-a-kind artist dolls. Alisa has an extensive network, which she utilizes in looking for retired items. Collectors should call the company with their requests. The firm also offers doll appraisals.

• • • • • • •

Alleans Collectables

Thieves Market
Corner of Ironwood and Edison
South Bend, IN 46635
Phone: 219/233-9820

Mailing Address:
29210 C.R. 10W.
Elkhart, IN 46514
Phone: 219/262-3338 - weekdays

- **Store Hours:** Saturday and Sunday: 10:00-6:00.

- **Secondary Market Lines:** Bradford Plates, Ashton-Drake, Rockwell, M.I. Hummel, Lladro, ANRI Woodcarvings, Jan Hagara, Maud Humphrey, All Schmid, Precious Moments.

- **Secondary Market Terms:** Consignment. Some buy outright. Trade. Layaways available.

- **Business History:** Collectors looking for an enjoyable weekend away from home, can browse for hours in a South Bend antique mall featuring 36 dealers, including some excellent jewelry dealers. Alleans Collectibles is located in this mall. In 1975, Allean Trafford started selling ANRI Woodcarvings and hasn't looked back. Her business is a Redemption Center for M.I. Hummel. Allean publishes an attractive newsletter and invites collectors to call or write to be placed on the mailing list. Collector searches are conducted by Allean, who thoroughly enjoys tracking down retired items. Collectors may also contact this firm for appraisals for insurance purposes.

• • • • • • •

All-Star Celebrity Collectibles

451 E. Main Street Suite #1
Ventura, CA 93001
Phone: 805/643-9224
Phone: 800/634-FANS
Fax: 805/659-5107

- **Store Hours:** Tuesday-Sunday: 11:00-5:00 or by appointment.

- **Secondary Market Lines:** Gartlan USA, Salvino, Sports Legends, Sports Impressions, Pro-Sport Creations, Hackett-American, USA Hartland, Star Company, Sports Collector's Warehouse, Bradford Exchange, Hamilton Collection, Ernst, Effanbee, World Doll, Expressive Designs, McCormick Distilling Company ("Elvis" bottles).

- **Secondary Market Terms:** Buy, sell or trade! Consignments considered. Call for details.

- **Business History:** All-Star Celebrity Collectibles features the largest sports and movie memorabilia inventory between Los Angeles and San Francisco. The store is celebrating its first anniversary, owned and operated by Mike Thomas, former radio station owner and long time collector. All-Star Celebrity Collectibles' specialty is sports and movie limited edition autographed and unsigned plates, figurines, balls, bats, dolls, steins and lithographs. The store manager, Bonnie Booth, contributes her artistic talents in the repair and restoration of damaged figurines, resulting in a recent appointment by Bob Gartlan, as the official West Coast figurine restoration center for Gartlan USA. Customers are invited to call toll-free for a free estimate on the repair of their limited edition figurines.

• • 3 • •

• • • • • • •

Amanda's Fine Gifts

279 Central Park Mall
San Antonio, TX 78216-5506
Phone: 512/525-0412
Phone: 800/441-4458

- **Store Hours:** Monday–Saturday: 10:00-9:00. Sunday: 12:00-6:00.

- **Secondary Market Lines:** Lladro, Swarovski, M.I. Hummel, Miss Martha's Originals, Tom Clark, Ron Lee, Armani, Chilmark, Sarah's Attic, Duncan Royale, Lowell Davis, Bossons.

- **Secondary Market Terms:** Consignments. Buy outright. Layaway.

- **Business History:** Barry Harris developed a deep appreciation for Lladro artwork, which eventually led to the purchase of Amanda's Fine Gifts in 1983. The store had actually opened in 1979, and its first manager, Julie Shaw, still works there today. Realizing the great potential for offering Lladro artwork and information to collectors, Barry and his staff have become known as experts in the field. The largest Lladro dealer in the southwest, Amanda's has welcomed Lladro family members to the store for artist appearances. Other guests have included Don Polland, Tom Clark, Ron Lee, Michael Boyett, Max Duncan and M.I. Hummel artists.

    Amanda's is a Redemption Center for Lladro, Swarovski, Tom Clark, Miss Martha's Originals, Ron Lee, Lalique, M.I. Hummel and Armani collector clubs. The store also offers an appraisal service for insurance purposes.

• • • • • • •

Armiks/Western States Trading Co.

18293 Soledad Canyon
Canyon Country, CA 91351
Phone: 805/298-5690

- **Store Hours:** Mondays only for after market inquiries.

- **Secondary Market Lines:** Legends, Chilmark, Bell Haven.

- **Secondary Market Terms:** Consignment: 20% net commission.

- **Business History:** Entrepreneur Cecil Comstock brings 38 years of collecting experience to his business. He is knowledgeable and articulate, able to educate collectors about the secondary market, as he assists them with their secondary market dealings.

  Comstock founded Western States Trading Co. in 1978, but has been active in the secondary market for 22 years. Today he owns three stores known as Armik's Fine Collectibles. He is one of the larger dealers in the country for Bell Haven and Legends, in addition to specializing in Chilmark for their mixed media and Civil War pieces. Armiks is also a Redemption Center for the Legends and Chilmark collector clubs.

• • • • • • •

Atlanta Exchange

4740 Matthews Park
Snellville, GA 30278
Phone: 404/979-4638
Phone: 800 line for sellers/subscribers

- **Store Hours:** Monday–Friday: 9:00-6:00. Sat.: 9:00-12 noon.

- **Secondary Market Lines:** Department 56, Tom Clark, David Winter, M.I. Hummel, Precious Moments, Lilliput Lane, Royal Doulton, Cat's Meow, Maud Humphrey, Lladro, Disney, Swarovski, Lowell Davis, Hallmark, Goebel, Wee Forest Folk, Rockwell, Sports Impressions, plates, dolls, Krystonia, ANRI, Memories of Yesterday, Whitley Bay, Duncan Royale, Lefton.

- **Secondary Market Terms:** Sellers send in listings of their own pieces for sale. A 10% commission is added at the time of the sale to the buyer, plus applicable shipping charges. When a buyer calls, he is quoted the lowest price for that day. If accepted, the buyer sends his payment to the Exchange, and the item is then ordered from the seller. The item is inspected by the Exchange and shipped to the buyer. Three days are granted upon arrival for buyer inspection/approval. The seller is then paid. Exchange also has "Collectible Consignment Corner" available for in-store purchasing. Call for details.

- **Business History:** The Atlanta Exchange publishes a 15-20 page monthly newsletter which includes collectibles news and history, concentrating on Department 56! An extensive secondary price listing is included to connect buyers and sellers, trades and a source for locating missing parts, boxes, etc. Newsletters run $24.00 annually for 12 issues. The Exchange has a convenient layaway plan to help buyers. Please call for details. Owner, Peggy Pridgen, invites collectors to enjoy "Southern Hospitality" today!

A Work of Art

7-11 Legion Drive
Valhalla, NY 10595
Phone: 914/948-4655 (office)
Phone: 800/552-3766 (technical & warehouse)
Fax: 914/948-4367

- **Office Hours:** Monday–Friday: 9:00-6:00.

- **Secondary Market Lines:** Lladro.

- **Secondary Market Terms:** Subscription to publication: one year-$24, two years-$45. Sales of pieces: outright or layaway. Call for details. Purchases of pieces: outright

- **Business History:** A Work of Art has been in business since 1990 and is recognized by many as one of the best authorities for the Lladro secondary market. The firm publishes *A Work of Art*, a publication solely about the Lladro secondary market. It provides current values, histories of pieces, auction results and other essential information for collectors that is not available elsewhere.

  Brad Welch, technical vice-president, posseses considerable information about the retired Lladro line and can assist collectors in identifying Lladro artwork and locating retired figurines. A Work of Art buys and sells pieces at fair prices. The company has accumulated a large inventory of retired pieces.

  The A Work of Art staff is available to counsel subscribing collectors on matters related to retired Lladros.

• • • • • • •

B.J. Dolls & Gifts

P.O. Box 1481-6
Brockton, MA 02403
Phone: 508/586-1279

- **Store Hours:** Daily: 8:00am-11:00pm by phone.

- **Secondary Market Lines:** Department 56, Hallmark, David Winter, June McKenna, Madame Alexander dolls, Barbies, Jem dolls, Muffy Vanderbears, plus more!

- **Secondary Market Terms:** Consignments. Buy outright. Exchange service. Layaways.

- **Business History:** Barbara Jo McKeon has been selling dolls, other limited edition collectibles and books for sixteen years. She is the author of rare and hard-to-find Madame Alexander collector dolls and Madame Alexander catalog reprints. She has been exhibiting at doll and collectible shows all over the United States and is a promoter of collectibles shows. B.J. Dolls & Gifts maintains a "wish list" for collectors seeking retired items. Barbara considers herself very successful at locating these items and invites collectors to contact her with their requests.

The Baggage Car

513 Elm St., PO Box 65485
West Des Moines, IA 50265
Phone: 515/255-3070

- **Store Hours:** Monday–Friday: 11:00-5:00. Other times, by appointment.

- **Secondary Market Lines:** Hallmark: Ornaments, Merry Miniatures, Pins, Little Gallery, Cookie Cutters, Stocking Hangers, Magnets, Dolls, Table Decorations (Other than paper), Enesco Ornaments and Miniatures.

- **Secondary Market Terms:** No consignments. Buy outright. Call for details.

- **Business History:** The Baggage Car, founded in 1977, was originally an antique store. In 1979, owner Meredith DeGood began to carry the Hallmark cloth dolls. When she learned in early 1982 about the introduction of a collector's guide on the Hallmark Keepsake Ornaments, she was convinced that she should concentrate on amassing a large inventory of ornaments. The firm began publishing lists of its merchandise for collectors in the United States and Canada. Soon, she began publishing five lists per year, along with a newsletter. Almost 97% of the business is conducted by mail. Husband Hal joined Meredith in 1987.

  The Baggage Car merchandise list is often accepted for insurance purposes, and the price guide is one of the most complete in the field. Meredith attends many ornament conventions, often speaking on this subject.

• • • • • •

Barbara's

448 W. Solomon St.
Griffin, GA 30223
Phone: 404/229-6249

- **Store Hours:** Monday–Friday: 9:00-6:00. Saturday: 10:00-5:00.

- **Secondary Market Lines:** Cat's Meow, Sheila's Houses, Sarah's Attic, Lilliput Lane, Ray Day prints, S.A.M.'s Designs (corn-husk dolls), John Sandridge prints, Lovelife collectibles, Attic Babies, Constance Collection, Town Square Village.

- **Secondary Market Terms:** Some buy outright. Consignments. Trades. Layaways available. Will do searches for Cat's Meow pieces.

- **Business History:** Just prior to 1987, Barbara Entrekin was stricken with cancer and thought she had one year to live. She decided to spend that year doing something she had always dreamt of undertaking -- starting her own business. Today, Barbara's (and Barbara!) are thriving. The store carries a delightful selection of Cat's Meow pieces, in addition to many other unique gift and collectibles items. In addition to the lines above, Barbara's carries Rowe pottery, Boyd's Bears, Lange calendars, Colonial Village lighted Christmas houses by Lefton and is a consultant for Longaberger baskets. Many of these intricately woven baskets are on display, including signed and dated pieces. Barbara's also markets attractive gourmet food baskets, which are created and then shipped worldwide. The store holds an open house each Thanksgiving weekend and is also a Redemption Center for the Cat's Meow collectors club and Glynda Turley prints.

Barbara's Gatlinburg Shops

Barbara's Elegants
John Cody Gallery
511, 716, 963 Parkway
Gatlinburg, TN 37738
Phone: 800/433-1132

- **Store Hours:** Daily: 9:00-9:00.

- **Secondary Market Lines:** Chilmark, Hudson, Tom Clark, David Winter, Lladro, Swarovski, Wee Forest Folk, Krystonia, Lilliput Lane, Department 56: Snow Village and Snowbabies, Byers' Choice, Sandicast, All God's Children, Maud Humphrey, Cades Cove Cabin, Cody limited edition prints.

- **Secondary Market Terms:** Call for details.

- **Business History:** Barbara Beville has been active in the collectibles field since 1975. She is one of the largest volume dealers in eastern Tennessee. In addition to the store listed above, Barbara owns two additional stores in Gatlinburg, Barbara's Elegants at 716 Parkway and the Gatlinburg Shop at 963 Parkway.

  Members of NALED, the stores are also Redemption Centers for Chilmark, Hudson, Tom Clark, David Winter, Lladro, Swarovski, Krystonia, Lilliput Lane and All God's Children collector clubs. Artist appearances are scheduled throughout the year at all of the shops. Newsletters are mailed ten to twelve times annually, highlighting recent product releases and collector club news.

• • • • • • •

Best Collectibles

Hwy 60 South
P.O. Box 152
Morganton, GA 30560
Phone: 706/838-5920

- **Store Hours:** 24-hour call service.

- **Secondary Market Lines:** Department 56: Snow Village, New England Village, Alpine Village, Dickens Village, Christmas in the City, Snowbabies, cold casts, lite-ups, Snow Village and Heritage Village accessories; David Winter, Duncan Royale, Maud Humphrey, Tom Clark Gnomes, Windy Meadows, Memories of Yesterday, Legends, Lilliput Lane, Byer's Choice, Armani, Rockwell.

- **Secondary Market Terms:** 15% commission. Includes shipping and handling to the buyer. Call for details.

- **Business History:** Best Collectibles was established in 1990 as an exchange and mail order service. This firm is the only secondary market exchange service in the North Georgia Mountains. Their slogan is "BEST cure for COL-LECTIBLE-itis."

  "Best Collectibles", a bi-monthly publication is available to collectors on a three-month trial basis for $10.00 or annually for $18.00. Collectors are updated on various collectibles, in addition to the listing of retired artwork for sale by other collectors.

  Owner, Linda Ross is also a monthly contributor to the *Mountain Review Magazine* and a member of Prodigy.

• • • • • • •

Biggs Limited Editions

5517 Lakeside Avenue
Richmond, VA 23228
Phone: 800/637-0704
Fax: 804/266-7775

- **Store Hours:** Monday-Saturday: 9:00-9:00. Sunday: 1230-5:30.

- **Secondary Market Lines:** Dolls: Ashton-Drake, Bello, Gadco; Figurines: David Winter, June McKenna, Swarovski.

- **Secondary Market Terms:** No consignment. May buy outright. Layaway available.

- **Business History:** Biggs Limited Editions was started by Donny Biggs, who began collecting in 1982, and had difficulty locating a collectibles store near his home. He enjoyed his hobby so much, that he opened his own collectibles store in 1985.

  Biggs Limited Editions is a very attractive store, which acts as a Redemption Center for many major lines. Collectibles are displayed in unique settings, often in separate rooms. The pewter and dolls galleries are particularly striking.

  Open houses and artist appearances are held three or four times annually. Collectors are often able to buy their artwork signed by an artist who has previously visited the store – at no additional cost. The store also offers free shipping in the continental U.S. Satisfaction is always guaranteed at Biggs.

•   •   •   •   •   •   •

Blevins Plates 'n' Things

301 Georgia St.
Vallejo, CA 94590
Phone: 707/642-7505
Phone: 800/523-5511

Blevins Plates 'n' Things
Collectors Plates, Figurines, Dolls, etc.

- **Store Hours:** Monday–Friday: 10:00-6:00. Saturday: 9:00-5:00. Closed Sunday.

- **Secondary Market Lines:** Bradford plates, Hamilton plates, Memories of Yesterday, Lowell Davis, David Winter, Lilliput Lane, Sports Impressions, Precious Moments, Enchantica, Swarovski, Goebel Miniatures, Flambro, ANRI, Jan Hagara, Ashton-Drake dolls, Maud Humphrey, lithographs.

- **Secondary Market Terms:** Outright buy on Ashton-Drake dolls. No consignment. Call for details.

- **Business History:** Blevins Plates 'n' Things has grown from an in-home business to a 4,000 square foot store over a period of ten years. The owners are Larry and Stella Blevins. Years of selling have brought knowledge to the owners and staff. A member of NALED, Blevins is a Redemption Center for numerous collector clubs and hosts artist open houses during the year. They also offer layaways and do a brisk mail order business.

The Blossom Shop

112 N. Main
Farmer City, IL 61842
Phone: 800/842-2593

- **Store Hours:** Monday-Wednesday and Friday: 8:00-4:00.
  Thursday and Saturday: 8:00-12:00.

- **Secondary Market Lines:** Sebastian Miniature figurines.

- **Secondary Market Terms:** Consignment. Buy outright.
  Call for details.

- **Business History:** Owner Jim Waite acquired The Blossom
  Shop in 1974 as a retail florist. In 1979, he added collectible lines to
  his business and became particularly interested in Sebastian
  Miniatures. Today, Jim is one of the country's foremost experts on
  the Sebastian line and matches buyers and sellers who collect these
  pieces. He is willing to search for Sebastian Miniatures and keeps a
  list of what collectors want to buy and sell. Collectors are informed
  as private editions become available. A Redemption Center for the
  Sebastian Miniature Collectors Society, The Blossom Shop also offers
  an appraisal service for collectors to insure their ever-expanding collection.

  Jim Waite is the sponsor of the Midwest Sebastian Fair that originat-
  ed in 1981. The fair is held in October each year and features many
  activities, including a look alike contest, and a premier auction of
  rare miniatures. Secondary market dealers are also invited to set up
  to sell retired Sebastian Miniatures. Three private commissions have
  been done specifically for The Blossom Shop in conjunction with the
  Sebastian Studios. Jim has also worked with many other organizations, promoting Sebastian Miniatures as fundraisers.

Bodzer's Collectibles

White Marsh Mall
8200 Perry Hall Blvd.
Baltimore, MD 21236
Phone: 410/931-9222

- **Store Hours:** Monday-Saturday: 10:00-9:30. Sunday: 11:00-5:00.

- **Secondary Market Lines:** Department 56, David Winter, M.I. Hummel, All God's Children, Maruri, Bradford plates, Ashton-Drake dolls, Rockwell figurines, Krystonia, Hamilton Collection, Legends, Maud Humphrey.

- **Secondary Market Terms:** No consignments. Buy outright.

- **Business History:** Bodzer's has been located at White Marsh Mall since 1982. A family owned business, they tripled the store size in 1990. Top of the line collectibles are attractively displayed, and the staff is knowledgeable. In addition, there is always a Bodzer on the floor.

  Steve, Dolly and son, Tony, love the business. Tony will take command of the firm by 1994. As Tony says, "the most important thing we sell is service!"

• • • • • • •

Boston Pewter Co.

5 S. Market Faneuil Marketplace
Boston, MA 02109
Phone: 617/523-1776

- **Store Hours:** Monday–Saturday: 10:00-9:00. Sunday: 12:00-6:00.

- **Secondary Market Lines:** Chilmark and Legends.

- **Secondary Market Terms:** Either buy outright or commission. Call for details.

- **Business History:** Located in historic Boston and specifically in Faneuil Marketplace, is the Boston Pewter Co., featuring one of the largest selections of American made pewter anywhere. Owner, Jeff Allen, opened Boston Pewter in 1987. The store carries handmade copper weathervanes, handblown glass, Hudson fantasy figurines and a stunning selection of Chilmark and Legends figurines. Boston Pewter, one of the largest dealers in the area for both Chilmark and Legends, is a Redemption Center for both collector clubs.

  Jeff Allen has been active in the secondary market since 1987 and actively seeks retired pieces on behalf of collectors looking for Chilmark and Legends artwork.

• • • • • • •

The Bradford Exchange

9333 N. Milwaukee Avenue
Niles, IL 60648
Phone: 800/323-8078
Phone: 708/966-1900 (in Illinois)

- **Hours:** Monday–Friday: 8:00-5:30.

- **Secondary Market Lines:** Collector's plates.

- **Secondary Market Terms:** The Bradford Exchange matches buyers with sellers by phone or mail. Buyers pay a 4% commission (or $4.00 if the price of the plate is under $100). Sellers are charged a 30% commission.

- **Business History:** Founded in 1973, The Bradford Exchange was the first entity to offer an organized secondary market for collector's plates. In 1982, Bradford's computerized Instaquote™ system went into effect, allowing the exchange to electronically match plate buyers with plate sellers from around the country. Bradford tracks the trading activity of more than 2,000 plates listed on the U.S. exchange, one of 11 offices around the world. Brokers can also help collectors to buy and sell some 8,000 other plates which are not listed.

  Buy or sell orders can be entered on the exchange by phone or by mail. Bradford guarantees that once the exchange notifies both parties that a match has occurred, the buyer is guaranteed delivery of a mint-condition plate at the confirmed price, and the seller is guaranteed payment of the confirmed price once his plate has been certified as mint condition.

Brewhaus™ Gift Shop

2622 N. East St.
Lansing, MI 48906
Phone: 517/484-4417
Phone: 800/359-3414 (To order)
Fax: 517/484-5212

- **Store Hours:** Monday, Tuesday, Thursday, Friday: 10:00-6:00. Wednesday: 12:00-6:00. Saturday: 10:00-5:00.

- **Secondary Market Lines:** Anheuser-Busch, Miller, Coors, Strohs, Old Style, Pabst, Hamms, Lone Star and other Brewery; steins, plates, truck banks and other collectibles, plus a full line of brewerey promotional items.

- **Secondary Market Terms:** Buy outright or trade. Call for details.

- **Business History:** In business since 1984, the Brewhaus™ Gift Shop specializes in officially licensed brewery promotional and collectible items. They are currently the licensee for the Lone Star stein program. They produce a bimonthly publication called *Stein Hotline* which is sent free to stein collectors. The firm also produces the "Collector's Connection Newsletter," a quarterly publication containing information about current issue and past issue steins and stein collecting in general. A stein photo album is also available, featuring over 600 color photos of past and current steins. Other color catalogs of brewery items are also available. Collectors are invited to call for current values, to trade or sell their steins on the Brewhaus™ free hotline. The company is one of the first and only companies to sell the promotional and collectible items of all the major and smaller breweries in a catalog program.

• • • • • • •

Buchanan Place

4642 Akron Rd.
Smithville, OH 44677
Phone: 216/669-3911
Fax: 216/669-3733

- **Store Hours:** Monday–Thursday: 8:00-8:00. Friday-Saturday: 8:00-9:00. Sunday: 12:30-5:30.

- **Secondary Market Lines:** Tom Clark Creations, Cat's Meow, All God's Children.

- **Secondary Market Terms:** No consignments.

- **Business History:** Founded in 1982, Buchanan Place specializes in the secondary market for the lines listed above, including, working locally and through mail order to meet customers' needs.

  Included in their Cat's Meow secondary market offerings, they host their own Cat's Meow club with special member benefits. They keep members informed through "Meow Grams" and newsletters. Buchanan Place also keeps a large inventory of retired gnomes.

The Calico Cat

5101 E. Busch Blvd.
Tampa, FL 33617
Phone: 813/988-0481
Fax: 813/622-7505

 CALICO CAT
Country And More...

- **Store Hours:** Monday–Saturday: 10:00-6:00. Thursday evening until 8:00. Sunday: 12:30-5:00.

- **Secondary Market Lines:** Department 56: Dickens, Snowbabies; Duncan Royale, Sarah's Attic, All God's Children, June McKenna, Miss Martha's Collection, Maud Humphrey, Vallaincourt Folk Art, Tom Clark Gnomes, Enesco ornaments, Byers' Choice, Simpich Carolers and Santas.

- **Secondary Market Terms:** Consignment or buy out-right. Call 813/621-8470 for details.

- **Business History:** In business since 1972, The Calico Cat is a browser's delight -- a small town atmosphere with a warm feeling. There are three stores located in the Tampa area, the one listed above, and the others located at 14434 N. Dale Mabry in Tampa and at 716 W. Lumsden in Brandon.

  Owner, Susan Clark, shops the U.S. for the latest in one-of-a-kind gift items, including handcrafted merchandise, Amish quilts, limited edition prints and folk art. Each store also carries Tampa Bay's largest selection of counted cross stitch supplies.

Callahan's Of Calabash

Beach Road
Route 7, Box 302
Calabash, NC 28467
Phone: 800/344-3816

- **Store Hours:** Daily: 9:30-10:00-Summer, Winter- 9:30-9:00.

- **Secondary Market Lines:** All Department 56 villages and accessories, Tom Clark Creations, Lilliput Lane, Wee Forest Folk, Krystonia. Will accept other viable retired collectibles as well.

- **Secondary Market Terms:** This establishment is happy to accept listings of a viable retired collectible and advertise them in their collectible newsletter, which is mailed monthly to subscribers throughout the United States. There is no charge for listing. A 15% commission is passed on to sellers upon the sale of their collectible. Call for more details.

- **Business History:** Callahan's of Calabash grew from a small nautical gift shop at the northern end of the Myrtle Beach Grand Strand, to a 20,000 square foot store, featuring excellent collectible lines, with many retired pieces on display. The store includes St. Nick Nacks, the area's largest Christmas shop, an Easter shop, Halloween room and so very much more. Over 100,000 people visit the store each year!

• • • • • • •

Carol's Cards & Gifts

5285 West 95th Street
Overland Park, KS 66207
Phone: 913/642-8850
Fax: 913/642-5482

- **Store Hours:** Monday–Saturday: 9:00-5:30.

- **Secondary Market Lines:** Memories of Yesterday,
  Laura's Attic, Precious Moments figurines, Precious Moments
  Christmas, Swarovski, Enesco Musicals, Nao by Lladro.

- **Secondary Market Terms:** Consignments. Buy outright.

- **Business History:** In 1985, Carol and Leonard Glass
  opened Carol's Cards & Gifts. Today, the store is bustling
  with activity, as it is a Redemption Center for Enesco,
  Memories of Yesterday and Swarovski, and sponsors two
  Precious Moments and two Memories of Yesterday events
  annually. The store also carries two new lines: Cherished
  Teddies and Sugar Town. Carol's offers free out-of-state
  shipping and complimentary gift-wrapping.

  Collectors may call or fax to be placed on the mailing list for
  Carol's newsletter. The store also offers a search service for
  interested collectors who are seeking retired pieces.

Carol's Crafts

125 S. Van Buren Street
P.O. Box 960
Nashville, IN 47448
Phone: 812/988-6388

**CAROL'S
CRAFTS**

- **Store Hours:** Daily: 10:00-5:00.

- **Secondary Market Lines:** Goebel Miniatures, ANRI, Lilliput Lane, Lowell Davis.

- **Secondary Market Terms:** Buy/Sell brokerage.

- **Business History:** Carol's Crafts was founded in 1972, strictly as a craft supply shop. Today, the 2,000 square-foot facility houses gifts and collectibles, including a large selection of each collectible line carried and dollhouses and miniatures.

  Owners, Dave and Carol Derbyshire and their knowledgeable staff are ready to assist collectors in their primary or secondary market purchases. The store features beautiful displays of several primary lines, including ANRI Woodcarvings, Goebel Miniatures, Lilliput Lane cottages, Lowell Davis, Sarah's Attic, Enesco's Action Musicals, Memories of Yesterday, Possible Dreams Clothtique Santas, Snowbabies, Laura's Attic and Miss Martha's Originals.

  The Derbyshires mail customized newsletters geared toward collectors' prior collectible purchases, keeping them informed of the latest product introductions. Open houses and artist appearances are also hosted by the store.

• • • • • • •

Carol's Gift Shop

17601 So. Pioneer Blvd.
Artesia, CA 90701
Phone: 310/924-6335   Carol's Gift Shop
Fax: 213/924-2677   Collector's Corner

- **Store Hours:** Monday-Thursday: 9:30-5:30. Friday: 9:30-7:00. Saturday: 9:30-5:30.

- **Secondary Market Lines:** Department 56, Swarovski, Lowell Davis, Precious Moments, M.I. Hummel, ANRI, Wee Forest Folk, Lladro, graphics and collector plates.

- **Secondary Market Terms:** Buy outright or very generous trade.

- **Business History:** Established in 1958, Carol's Gift Shop features nearly all major collector lines. A full-service and complete Bradford retailer, the store is also a Distinguished Service Center for Precious Moments, in addition to sponsoring the Something Special Precious Moments Club. Carol's Gift Shop is a Redemption Center for more than 30 collector clubs.

Owner, Marge Rosenberg is considered one of the pioneers in the collectibles retail field. She is a charter member of NALED. She is also a charter member of the country's oldest plate club, the International Plate Collector's Guild and has served on its board for twenty years. Over the years, Mrs. Rosenberg has been a contributing writer to several collectible publications, including her present position as a columnist for *Collectors Mart* magazine.

Carousel Collectibles

P.O. Box 97172
Pittsburgh, PA 15229
Phone: 412/367-2352

- **Store Hours:** 9:00-9:00 daily.

- **Secondary Market Lines:** Hallmark: Christmas, Easter and miniature ornaments, Merry Miniatures and more.

- **Secondary Market Terms:** Buy outright.

- **Business History:** Joan Ketterer is the owner of Carousel Collectibles. Her admiration for Hallmark products led her to write contemporary greeting cards on a free-lance basis for Hallmark in the 1960s. In the 1970s, she was the first in line to buy the ornaments, and in the 1980s, in addition to writing two columns for collectible publications, she started her company. Carousel Collectibles is a secondary market dealership based on offering mint condition ornaments at competitive prices. A copy of Joan's 30-page price list is available for $3.00.

  In 1989, Joan began publishing her very popular newsletter, "Twelve Months of Christmas." It is published 23 times per year at an annual subscription price of $32.20 and keeps long-time and new collectors informed about the new product line, and provides a secondary market report, local show news, local club information, personality profiles and general Hallmark tips. A sample copy is available by sending a self-addressed stamped envelope. Late breaking Hallmark information can be obtained by calling 900/988-0023, Ext. 828 for $2.00 per minute. Touch tone is required, and callers must be at least eighteen.

• • • • • • •

Becky Carter, Inc.

9605 Red Bird Lane
Alpharetta, GA 30202
Phone: 404/475-8138

- **Hours:** Days: Answering service. Evenings until 9:00.

- **Secondary Market Lines:** Department 56: all villages, accessories, ornaments, snowglobes.

- **Secondary Market Terms:** Buy outright. Trading. Locator service.

- **Business History:** A collector of Department 56, Becky Carter started her business in 1988, exhibiting at local collector shows. Today, Becky has expanded her business, offering information and quality service to collectors, as she exhibits nationwide. She is able to offer expert advice to Department 56 collectors because of her extensive knowledge about the line. She, herself, owns every piece of the Heritage Village. In fact, a local television station featured Becky's collection, whose set was built by her husband. Becky Carter, Inc. is a full-service collectibles exchange for Department 56 items, where buying, selling and trading occurs daily. Becky keeps current on Department 56 products and news and shares this with collectors. She advises collectors on how to insure their collectibles and has consulted between insurance companies and collectors regarding claims. Becky is also knowledgeable about variations and proofs. Becky Carter, Inc.. guarantees customer satisfaction. The price quoted by the firm on any retired piece is the final price, including shipping. If for any reason an item must be returned, the company pays the shipping cost -- a benefit not always offered to collectors by other secondary market businesses.

Charity's Gift Shop

105 Guilbeau Road
Lafayette, LA 70506
Phone: 318/981-1460

- **Store Hours:** Monday–Saturday: 9:30-6:00. Collectors may call until 10:00pm.

- **Secondary Market Lines:** Precious Moments, Lowell Davis, Tom Clark Gnomes, Memories of Yesterday, Sarah's Attic, All God's Children, M.I. Hummel, Maud Humphrey, Jan Hagara, Bessie Pease Gutmann, ANRI, Granget ducks, David Winter, Lladro, Emmett Kelly.

- **Secondary Market Terms:** Consignments. Buy outright. Trade.

- **Business History:** Charity's Gift Shop owner, Charity Marie Dupuis, started her business in 1974 because she loved figurines. Today, Charity -- and Charity's -- are still going strong! Collectors are invited to experience the inviting atmosphere and activities hosted by this firm.

  The largest collectibles store in Lafayette, Charity's is a Distinguished Service Retailer for Precious Moments and holds two events annually in honor of this collectibles line. They also have four to five open houses or artist appearances every year, including a week-long special event in the fall. The store is a Redemption Center for numerous collector clubs. Charity Dupuis always enjoys meeting the artists and discovering the story behind each collectible, which she shares with her customers. She offers an appraisal service and does free shipping on orders of $75 or more.

• • • • • • •

Cheerios

Emerald Square Mall
999 S. Washington Street
North Attleboro, MA 02760
Phone: 508/643-1174

- **Store Hours:** Monday-Saturday: 10:00-9:30. Sunday: 12:00-6:00.

- **Secondary Market Lines:** David Winter, Byers' Choice, Swarovski, Department 56: no Christmas in the City; June McKenna, Miss Martha's Originals, Tom Clark Gnomes, Lilliput Lane, Lladro, Lowell Davis, Emmett Kelly, Jr., M.I. Hummel, Wee Forest Folk.

- **Secondary Market Terms:** Consignment. Buy outright. Call for details.

- **Business History:** Originally from London, England, Kip Patel purchased Cheerio's in 1985, shortly after he moved to the States. Already in existence since 1942, the store now features collectibles and some giftware. Today, Cheerios has five locations to serve the collector. Collectors calling any one of the stores will immediately notice the host of English accents – all relatives of Kip!

  Cheerio's provides prompt, friendly service. The store is a Redemption Center for John Hine, Miss Martha's Originals, Swarovski, Precious Moments, Chilmark, Lladro, Lilliput Lane, Legends, M.I. Hummel and Lowell Davis. Open houses and artist appearances are held frequently.

  Active on the secondary market, Cheerios is happy to locate hard-to-find pieces.

• • • • • • •

Cherry Tree Cards & Gifts Inc.

11200 Scaggsville Road
Laurel, MD 20723
Phone: 301/498-8528

- **Store Hours:** Monday-Friday: 10:00-9:00. Saturday: 10:00-7:00. Sunday: 12:00-5:00.

- **Secondary Market Lines:** Precious Moments, M.I. Hummel and more.

- **Secondary Market Terms:** Buy outright.

- **Business History:** Father and daughter team, Earl Seth and Diane Hild, opened Cherry Tree Cards & Gifts Inc. in 1990. Although the store carries greeting cards, photo albums, balloons, calligraphy prints and gift wrap, Cherry Tree is best known for its excellent selection of collectibles. They have one of the largest Precious Moments and Hummel displays in the area. They also carry Cat's Meow, Tom Clark Gnomes, Lucy & Me, David Winter, Lilliput Lane, Musical Showcase, Growing Up Girls, Miss Martha's Originals, Memories of Yesterday, Maud Humphrey, Emmett Kelly, Jr., Annalee Mobilitee, Melodies in Motion, Sarah's Attic, Ginny dolls and limited edition plates. A member of NALED, Cherry Tree is also a Redemption Center for most major collector clubs. Several special events are organized and hosted annually. One such event planned is a sales representative day, with all lines represented and experts on hand to answer collectors' questions. A newsletter is published bi-monthly, available to collectors. The Cherry Tree sales staff are all collectors, friendly and knowledgeable -- ready to serve and educate the customer.

The Christmas Shop
Tepeetown, Inc.

12 Castillo Drive
St. Augustine, FL 32084
Phone: 904/824-9898
Fax: 904/829-8555

- **Store Hours:** Daily: 9:30-6:00.

- **Secondary Market Lines:** M.I. Hummel, Lladro, Precious Moments, Department 56, Chilmark, Duncan Royale, David Winter, Lilliput Lane, Lowell Davis, Perillo, De Grazia, Goebel, Alexander dolls, Cairn Studios: Tom Clark.

- **Secondary Market Terms:** Consignment. Buy outright--"paid" in cash or merchandise.

- **Business History:** Tepeetown and The Christmas Shop was founded in 1945 and is under the private ownership of the Harris family. In the retail business since 1945, President and C.E.O. Frederick Harris' numerous gift shops specialize in fine gifts and collectibles. He has served on advisory boards for major companies such as Goebel for the M.I. Hummel line, The Lance Corp. producing Chilmark Pewter Sculpture and Royal Doulton's fine bone china.

Well versed on both the primary and secondary markets for all collectible lines carried, the entire staff provides effective aftermarket assistance, with an ever-expanding client base throughout the United States and abroad. Several in-store events are planned throughout each year. The business now boasts the employ of the third generation "Harris" and assures future credibility for the firm and their customers.

Christmas In Vermont

RD #1, Box 1895
Barre, VT 05641
Phone: 802/479-2024

- **Hours:** Daily: 9:00-9:00.

- **Secondary Market Lines:** Hallmark: Christmas ornaments, Light & Motion, Miniature and Collectible series ornaments, Limited and Special Edition ornaments and Merry Miniatures; limited line of Enesco and Carlton.

- **Secondary Market Terms:** Buy outright.

- **Business History:** Kathy Parrott, owner of Christmas In Vermont, runs a rapidly growing predominantly Hallmark mail order business which has many satisfied customers throughout the United States and abroad. Every year, the firm's list of customers grows, because they specialize in giving fast, dependable and friendly service with competitive prices. They take great pride in maintaining a strict policy of selling only mint condition ornaments. They ship first class mail the day after an order is received and also offer overnight Express mail on request. In addition , the firm offers a service for locating hard-to-find ornaments in the event they are out of a particular item. Christmas In Vermont was honored in a one-page article which appeared in the December 1991 edition of *Twelve Months of Christmas*. The firm advertises in the *Antique Trader, Collectors Mart, Southern Antiques* and *Collectors News*. A complete 22-page price list is available by sending $1.00 along with a self-addressed stamped business size envelope with 52 cents postage.

• • • • • • •

Classic Cargo

5494 E. Highway 98
Destin, FL 32541
Phone: 904/837-8171
Phone: 800/833-8171
Fax: 904/837-8955

- **Store Hours:** Daily: 10:00-9:00.

- **Secondary Market Lines:** Swarovski, All God's Children, David Winter, Lilliput Lane, Tom Clark Gnomes.

- **Secondary Market Terms:** Consignments. Buy outright. Buy/sell brokerage.

- **Business History:** Classic Cargo is a 2,400 square foot store in a large resort area on Gulf-to-Bay in Florida. Opened in 1981, Martha and Glenn Kilpatrick purchased the shop in 1989, and recently opened a second store. Today, Classic Cargo is a member of NALED and carries most major collectibles lines.

  The Kilpatricks call their store a "collectors paradise," because of their emphasis on excellent customer service. They publish a newsletter which highlights the collectibles market, including information on recent product releases. Collectors may call or write if they wish to be placed on the mailing list. Classic Cargo specializes in the Swarovski secondary market, which is covered extensively in the firm's newsletter.

• • • • • • •

Clemons-Eicken

At The Borgata
6166 N. Scottsdale Road #204
Scottsdale, AZ 85253
Phone: 602/998-9042

CLEMONS-EICKEN
Fine European Imports

- **Store Hours:** Monday–Saturday: 10:00-5:30.

- **Secondary Market Lines:** Boehm, Cybis, David
Winter Cottages, Lladro, Royal Doulton, Swarovski.

- **Secondary Market Terms:** Consignment. Buy outright.
Call for details.

- **Business History:** Founded in 1981, Clemons-Eicken
boasts one of the largest collections of Boehm, Cybis, Lladro
and Royal Doulton in Arizona.

  In addition to featuring the world's finest crystal and porcelain, Clemons-Eicken also serves as headquarters for the collectors societies of Armani, David Winter Cottages, Lladro,
Lalique, Royal Doulton, Mats Jonasson and Edna Hibel. All
of the above current members-only pieces are available, plus
issues from previous years.

  Clemons-Eicken also provides insurance appraisals for all
purchases of limited editions or rare sculptures. Vita R.
Clemons, owner, has extensive knowledge of both Boehm
and Cybis and serves as a contributing agent to the Boehm
Porcelain Society Advisory.

• • • • • • •

C-n-A Collectibles

17831 Fairwood Dr.
Fraser, MI 48026
Phone: 800/533-6760

- **Store Hours:** Monday–Friday: 9:00-9:00. Saturday: 9:00-2:00.

- **Secondary Market Lines:** Department 56: All villages; Swarovski, Memories of Yesterday, Lilliput Lane, David Winter, Lowell Davis, Emmett Kelly, Jr., Maud Humphrey, Precious Moments, Wee Forest Folk, Sports figures.

- **Secondary Market Terms:** Collectors are invited to simply call the exchange and ask for the piece they need. The company will then give the collector a quote on price and availability of the piece. There is a 20% commisssion included on each piece. When the collectible is received by C-n-A, they carefully inspect it for cracks and chips. When the purchaser has sent them his/her payment, the piece is then shipped to the buyer. The party has three days to inspect it and either keep it or return it to C-n-A. C-n-A stands behind each piece that leaves their exchange. They market each piece with an identifiable mark to ensure authenticity.

- **Business History:** C-n-A was established in 1991 and has expanded rapidly during this time. The firm will help collectors locate retired collectibles or sell their artwork, thereby saving them the time and phone calls necessary to complete each transaction.

••••••

Collectible Cottage

439 New Fieldstown Road
Gardendale, AL 35071
Phone: 205/631-2413
Fax: 205/631-0511

- **Store Hours:** Monday–Saturday: 10:00-5:30. Extended hours between Thanksgiving and Christmas.

- **Secondary Market Lines:** Tom Clark Gnomes, Swarovski, David Winter, Lladro, Lilliput Lane, Precious Moments, Bradford plates, Dolls: Madame Alexander, Annette Himstedt, Ashton-Drake; Memories of Yesterday, Maud Humphrey, Steiff, Legends, All God's Children, M.I. Hummel.

- **Secondary Market Terms:** Buy outright. Buy/sell brokerage - 25% commission. Layaway available.

- **Business History:** As a doll collector, Diane Hollis decided to turn her hobby into a business and established the Collectible Cottage in 1982. The store's original location was a lovely two-story cottage. A federal highway road change prompted a move a few years later to another site. The Collectible Cottage is a store bustling with activity. As a member of NALED and Gift Creations Concepts and a Bradford dealer, the business offers a wonderful selection of collectibles. Collectible Cottage is also a Showcase Dealer for Department 56. Customers attend annual open houses and receive lovely color catalogs featuring several lines. Diane Hollis opened a second store in 1985 at 141 Lorna Brook Village in Birmingham, Alabama 35216.

• • • • • • •

Collectible Exchange, Inc.

5466 Columbiana Road
New Middleton, OH 44442
Phone: 800/752-3208

- **Store Hours:** Daily: 9:00-10:00.

- **Secondary Market Lines:** All God's Children, ANRI, Armani, Byers' Choice, Cairn Gnomes, Chilmark, Cybis, Department 56, Duncan Royale, Emmett Kelly Jr., Enesco, Gartlan, Goebel Miniatures, Jan Hagara, Hallmark, Hamilton, John Hine Ltd., M.I. Hummel, Ispanky, June McKenna, Lefton, Legends, Lilliput Lane, Lladro, Lowell Davis, Maud Humphrey, Memories of Yesterday, Polland, Precious Moments, Raikes bears, Salvino, Sports Impressions, Swarovski, United Design, Wee Forest Folk, David Winter, Wysocki figurines, plus many doll and plate lines.

- **Secondary Market Terms:** Collectible Exchange, Inc. acts as a broker to protect the buyer and seller during a transaction. Collectible Exchange, Inc. lists items at no charge to the seller and adds a 20% brokerage fee.

- **Business History:** Collectible Exchange, Inc. is one of the world's largest secondary market brokers, offering service around the world and across the country. Having no affiliation with retail, they serve individuals, dealers and manufacturers. Buyers and sellers can deal with confidence, knowing that secondary market is their only business, not a sideline to a retail outlet. The firm offers low brokerage rates, satisfaction guaranteed, no subscription or membership fee, free price sheets and information.

• • • • • •

Collectible Express Ltd.

Division of Coast-to-Coast Connection: Midwest

2007 44 Street
Moline, IL 61265
Phone: 309/764-0378 (information)
Phone: 800/369-0085 (orders)

- **Store Hours:** Monday–Friday: 10:00-10:00. Saturday and Sunday: 8:00-12:00.

- **Secondary Market Lines:** Department 56, David Winter, Lilliput Lane, Swarovski, Lladro, Hummel, Precious Moments, Lowell Davis, Miss Martha's Originals, ANRI, Krystonia, Wee Forest Folk, Tom Clark, Jan Hagara, Duncan Royale, Ferrandiz, Sports figures, Armani, All God's Children, Christmas ornaments, Merry Miniatures, plates, Teddy bears, bells, lithographs and prints, dolls.

- **Secondary Market Terms:** Sellers send their item to the exchange when a prospective buyer is located. The item is inspected, then shipped to the interested party. Upon the buyer's acceptance, the exchange pays the seller. Free, no obligation listings and free price lists on request.

- **Business History:** Collectible Express Ltd. is part of an innovative group of three collectible exchanges spanning the country. Still keeping separate business names, these companies have merged under one singular service named "Coast-to-Coast-Connection." By calling one exchange, collectors can access information from all three. Owners, Nancy Romanot and Gayla Schaefer, provide secondary market services to collectors, having over 23 years of combined management and marketing experience. Their secondary market specialty is Department 56, among many other lines.

• • • • • • •

Collectible Finders Service

Division of Coast to Coast Connection: East

601 New Loudon Road, Suite 250
Latham, NY 12210
Phone: 800/524-6578
Fax: 800/524-6578

- **Hours:** Daily: 1:00-8:00. Fax anytime.

- **Secondary Market Lines:** Department 56, Armani, David Winter, Tom Clark Gnomes, Wee Forest Folk, Lilliput Lane, Swarovski, Maud Humphrey, ANRI, Krystonia, Duncan Royale, Lladro, Ferrandiz, Lowell Davis, Precious Moments, Miss Martha Originals, Sarah's Attic, lithos & prints, bears, dolls, plates.

- **Secondary Market Terms:** Free listings in newsletters. Broker's: 20%, including postage. Layaways accepted. No obligation. Dealers terms.

- **Business History:** Collectible Finders Service is part of an exciting concept called Coast to Coast Connection – three secondary market sources spanning the country, that offer the collector an excellent opportunity to buy and sell or trade their collectibles. They specialize in locating hard-to-find current collectibles, as well as retired and limited pieces. A bi-monthly newsletter is available to interested parties. The newsletter contains information on the latest pieces for sale.

  A relatively new business to the New York area, owner, Jeannette Conte, pledges that customer satisfaction is the firm's number one goal.

• • • • • • •

Collectible House

14855 Clayton Road
Chesterfield, MO 63017
Phone: 314/391-8755
Phone: 800/726-0440

"Collectors Serving Collectors"

- **Store Hours:** Monday–Friday: 9:00-9:00. Saturday: 9:00-6:00. Sunday: 11:00-5:00.

- **Secondary Market Lines:** Precious Moments, M.I. Hummel, David Winter, Swarovski, Hallmark, Enesco, Carlton ornaments, Lilliput Lane, Lowell Davis, Memories of Yesterday, Department 56, including Snowbabies and ornaments, Duncan Royale, Jan Hagara, including ornaments, and more.

- **Secondary Market Terms:** Buy outright. Consignments: 20% commission upon sale. 10% locator service. Call for details. Price lists upon request.

- **Business History:** Eileen Kaye opened Emily's Hallmark in 1983. Today, the store is one of the largest collectible ornament stores in the greater St. Louis area and a Gold Crown Hallmark store. Collectible House, a division of Emily's Hallmark, was begun in 1990 by Eileen and Michele Fenno in response to the demand by collectors for a secondary market vehicle. The firm publishes a price list and a newsletter called "Emily's Collectibles." The newsletter features product information, new product releases, lists of events and shows and a swap and sell section. The newsletter costs $12.00 annually, which includes two free ads. Special Artist's Events and Collector's Sundays are held throughout the year. The firm sponsors local collector clubs for ornaments, Precious Moments, Memories of Yesterday, David Winter and Lilliput Lane cottages and Department 56.

The Collectibles Corner

313 Alta Mesa Drive
So. San Francisco, CA 94080
Phone: 415/588-5595

The Collectibles Corner
LIMITED EDITIONS
PLATES, FIGURINES, COINS

- **Store Hours:** Tuesday–Thursday: 10:00-6:00. Friday-Sunday by appointment only. Closed Mondays.

- **Secondary Market Lines:** Plates: Rockwell, M.I. Hummel, Kuck, Perillo, DeGrazia, Zolan, Studio Dante, Bing & Grondahl, Royale Copenhagen and more; Figurines: M.I. Hummel, DeGrazia, Zolan, Kuck, Fontanini, Gutmann; lithographs, ornaments. Some dolls and bears.

- **Secondary Market Terms:** No consignments. Will accept lists and locate buyers. Mail and phone orders gladly accepted. Have large stock on hand, dating back 20 years or more!

- **Business History:** A collector herself for 25 years, owner Athalie ("Lee") Markowski opened The Collectibles Corner in 1979. She is a member of the International Guild and belongs to numerous collector clubs. She can assist collectors in redeeming their collector club exclusive pieces. Lee's extensive collectibles background is put to excellent use, as she matches buyers and sellers of collectibles. She does not charge for her research and answers all collectors' letters personally. Her motto -- "If it's advertised, I have it, or can get it!"

Collectibles etc., Inc.

8362 N. 49th Street
Brown Deer, WI 53223-3696   Collectibles etc., Inc.
Phone: 414/355-4545
Phone: 800/558-5594

- **Store Hours:** Monday–Saturday: Open 10:00am.

- **Secondary Market Lines:** Precious Moments, Ashton-Drake dolls, Hamilton dolls, plates, Rockwell, Perillo, Sandra Kuck, M.I. Hummel, Hallmark, houses and many others.....

- **Secondary Market Terms:** Collectibles etc., Inc.'s job is to MATCH buyers and sellers. They call their MATCH SERVICE the heartbeat of the booming secondary market. Using their Bid & Ask System, collectors' buy or sell requests can quickly be entered or matched like a stock market. It is the fast, easy and safe way to buy or sell. (They work with dealers too). Call for details and a complimentary newsletter.

- **Business History:** Founded in 1979 as a national mail order firm, Collectibles etc., Inc. ships worldwide. They also do appraisals and assist insurance and claims adjustors. According to owner Sandy Forgach, their firm "bends over backwards" to help you. "Try us, you will like us!"

  Collectibles etc., Inc. is ever-expanding and therefore expects to move soon. Collectors should call before visiting this store.

• • • • • • •

Collectibly Yours

43 E. Rt. 59
Spring Valley, NY 10977
Phone: 914/425-9244
Fax: 914/425-9244

• **Store Hours:** Tuesday-Saturday: 10:00-5:30. Sunday: By chance.

• **Secondary Market Lines:** Precious Moments, M.I. Hummel, Swarovski, Enesco Treasury ornaments, Lladro, Wee Forest Folk, Memories of Yesterday, Yolanda Bello, Ashton-Drake, Cabbage Patch, Himstedt, Dolls by Jerri, Gorham, Pat Thompson, Robin Woods, All God's Children, Bradford plates, Hamilton plates, Department 56: All villages and accessories, Snowbabies.

• **Secondary Market Terms:** Generally buy outright. Occasionally will consider consignment.

• **Business History:** Collectibly Yours is the largest collectible store in the area, including their extensive and beautiful selection of dolls. They are also a Showcase Dealer for Department 56.

Owner Rhea Milkes opened Collectibly Yours in 1978. A member of NALED and Gift Creations Concepts, the store is also a Redemption Center for Precious Moments, M.I. Hummel, Swarovski, Memories of Yesterday, Lladro and All God's Children.

Collectibly Yours sponsors the Department 56 Village Fever Collectors Club. Interested collectors should write or call.

• • • • • • •

Collections *Unlimited*

4867 1/2 Topanga Canyon Blvd.
Woodland Hills, CA 91364
Phone: 818/713-9390(24 hr.)
Call for 800 number to place orders only

COLLECTIONS *UNLIMITED*
UNIQUE *COLLECTIBLES* SINCE 1977

- **Store Hours:** Tuesday–Saturday: Noon-5:30. 24 hr. answering service, or by appointment.

- **Secondary Market Lines:** Department 56, Duncan Royale, Raikes Bears, Jan Hagara, Maud Humphrey, David Winter, Lilliput Lane, Ashton- Drake dolls, De Grazia, Sports Impressions, Incolay, Perillo, Redlin, Zolan, Kuck, Franca, Bannister, Stone. Extensive graphics and limited edition plates.

- **Secondary Market Terms:** Consignments. Buys outright sometimes. Free computerized brokerage service.

- **Business History:** "Serving collectors nationwide since 1977" is Collections Unlimited's tagline, offering collectors the opportunity to buy and sell wide ranges of collectibles.

  Owner Mickey Kaz typifies the spirit of collecting. In 1976, she began with one plate; a few years later, she had 300! Today, she uses her expertise and resources to match up buyers and sellers on a broad spectrum of artwork. Ms. Kaz's collectibles background is extensive. She managed popular plate artist, Nancy Turner, for a number of years. She was also one of the founders of the Valley Plate Club.

  Complimentary newsletters are available from Collections Unlimited, by sending a large stamped envelope.

Collector's Alley

108A S. Friendswood
Friendswood, TX 77546
Phone: 713/482-8238

 Collectors Alley

- **Store Hours:** Tuesday–Saturday: 11:30-6:30. Appointments before and after.

- **Secondary Market Lines:** All God's Children, Sarah's Attic, Tom Clark Gnomes, Madame Alexander Dolls, Real Musgrave dragons, North American Bears, Muffy and VIP Bears, Faithwick.

- **Secondary Market Terms:** Buy outright. Sell. Trade. Consignment. Layaways available. Keep search list particularly on dolls -- stays on until found. Layaways available.

- **Business History:** A collector "forever," Mary Kuhn joined a doll collectors club while living in New York and eventually opened her store in 1984, carrying one of the largest selections of dolls in the Houston area. In fact, the store is floor to ceiling dolls and bears from all over the world. Mary knows a host of doll artists and therefore keeps current on what's available in the market. She organizes about four open houses annually, including two doll artist appearances. The store is a Redemption Center for Tom Clark, Sarah's Attic, North American Bears and Real Musgrave. One of the annual highlights is the annual Girl Scout's day, where the scouts learn about doll collecting, working toward one of their badges. Mary shows her young guests a collection of Girl Scout dolls dating back to the early 1900s and provides a store tour. Collector's Alley also offers a doll repair service.

• • • • • •

Collector's Choice

4241 Boulder Ridge Point
Eagan, MN 55122
Phone: 612/454-1738

Collector's Choice
(Collectible Houses and Accessories)

- **Hours:** Monday–Saturday: 9:00-9:00.

- **Secondary Market Lines:** Department 56: All Villages and Accessories, Snowbabies; David Winter and more.

- **Secondary Market Terms:** Listing agent. Buyer pays 10% on top of asking price. Trades: split the commission.

- **Business History:** Kathy Bringewatt, a collector since 1984, kept very busy, between enjoying her hobby and her various careers. She spent five years in the retail field and taught elementary school for fifteen years. In early 1992, Kathy felt the need for a change and a new challenge. She had always wanted to be her own boss, and this dream became a reality, when she took her hobby and turned it into a business.

  Collector's Choice is off to an exciting and very successful start. This exchange began with about 300 listings and soon grew to 2,000. Kathy publishes a newsletter entitled "Collector's Choice," with subscriptions running $15.00 for 12 issues. This publication includes information on club meetings, Department 56 news, product releases, retirement announcements and special reports. And of course, each issue includes several pages of listings, allowing buyers and sellers to trade on the secondary market.

  Collector's Choice is expanding rapidly and expects to cover more lines each month. Collectors should call for details.

• • • • • • •

Collectors' Emporium

600 Meadowland Parkway
Secaucus, NJ 07094
Phone: 201/863-2977

COLLECTORS EMPORIUM
Collectibles & Fine Giftware

- **Store Hours:** Monday–Friday: 10:30-6:00. (5:00 July & August). Saturday: 10:00-6:00. Sunday: 12:00-5:00. Spring & Fall: Thursdays until 8:00.

- **Secondary Market Lines:** Department 56: Villages and Snowbabies; Swarovski, plates, Gartlan, Salvino, Sports Impressions, M.I. Hummel, Precious Moments, Ashton-Drake dolls.

- **Secondary Market Terms:** No consignments. Buy/sell outright.

- **Business History:** In the collectible business since 1977, the business was started as a mail order business, then expanded to exhibiting/selling at shows. In 1984, all operations were consolidated, and Collectors' Emporium opened its doors in a spacious 2,400 square-foot facility. They have been members of NALED almost since its inception.

The owners continue to seek out new and unusual products to present to their ever-expanding clientele, while maintaining a balance with the old, proven and established main collectible lines. They are designated as a Department 56 Showcase Dealer, sponsor numerous open house events and are a Redemption Center for most collector clubs. Their vast experience and knowledge give them the ability to help collectors seeking retired pieces. They also stand ready to purchase those items in demand by their customers.

• • • • • • •

Collectors Gallery & Landmark Collectors' Exchange

Oakdale Mall
7166 10th St. N., Box #8
Oakdale, MN 55128
Phone: 612/738-8351

Collectors Gallery &
Landmark Collectors'
Exchange

- **Store Hours:** Monday–Friday: 9:30-9:00. Saturday: 9:30-6:00. Sunday: 12:00-5:00.(Closed Sundays from Memorial Day-Labor Day)

- **Secondary Market Lines:** Department 56, Lladro, M.I. Hummel, Precious Moments, David Winter, Swarovski, Tom Clark Gnomes, Lilliput Lane, Armani, ANRI, Raikes Bears, and collector plates.

- **Secondary Market Terms:** Consignments. Outright purchase. Trade.

- **Business History:** Collectors Gallery first opened for business in 1981, owned and operated by Paul Runze and his son, Dan. Over the years, they have hosted numerous open houses featuring such famous names as Tom Clark, Giuseppe Armani, Gregory Perillo, David Tate, Ulrich Bernardi and many Hummel and David Winter touring artists. Collectors Gallery offers "full service" to the collector, including appraisals, locator service and nationwide shipping, as well as collector club headquarters for most top collector lines. The *Collectors Gallery Gazette* is issued periodically, and a Department 56 newsletter is published quarterly. The Landmark Collectors Exchange was recently formed to concentrate on the growing secondary market business.

Collector's Marketplace

RR 1 Box 213B
Montrose, PA 18801
Phone: 717/278-4094
Phone: 800/755-3123

- **Store Hours:** 24-hour secondary market service.

- **Secondary Market Lines:** Department 56, Swarovski, David Winter, Lilliput Lane, All God's Children, Jan Hagara, Maud Humphrey, Precious Moments, Lladro, M.I. Hummel, Steiff, United Design, Cat's Meow, ANRI, Lowell Davis, Constance Collection, Memories of Yesterday, Duncan Royale, Hallmark Ornaments, Enesco Ornaments, Steinbach & Ulbricht Nutcrackers, Dolls.

- **Secondary Market Terms:** No listing fees. Quoted price is the price buyer pays, plus shipping and handling. Shipped fully insured. Satisfaction completely guaranteed.

- **Business History:** Begun in 1989 as a response to their retail customers' interest in reselling and purchasing retired Department 56 pieces, Collector's Marketplace has grown from an instore service to a national secondary market source. Their success is directly attributed to the friendly, caring people who draw upon 20 years of collectible and giftware retail experience.

  As a Department 56 showcase dealer, the staff at Collector's Marketplace provide collectors with knowledgeable sales assistance on current releases. Their retail showroom, Cargo West Christmas Barn, is located in the Pocono Mountains of Pennsylvania on Route 611 in Scotrun, just off I-80. Collector's Marketplace is a member of NALED, Gift Association of America and Pennsylvania Retailers Association.

• • • • • • •

Collectors' Marketplace

Division of Coast-to-Coast Connection: West

N 8017 Hughes Drive
Spokane, WA 99208
Phone: 509/467-2300

- **Store Hours:** Monday–Saturday: 8:00-6:00 Pacific time.

- **Secondary Market Lines:** Department 56, David Winter, Lilliput Lane, Dolls, Raikes & Steiff bears, Plates, Lithos and Prints, Ornaments, Figurines: ANRI, Armani, DeGrazia, Duncan Royale, Ferrandiz, Gartlan, Goebel, Hagara, Hummel, Lladro, Maud Humphrey, Lowell Davis, McKenna, Salvino, Tom Clark Gnomes, Wee Forest Folk.

- **Secondary Market Terms:** Since January, 1991, this exchange has published a monthly newsletter in which subscribers may list the items they wish to sell, buy or trade. Sellers send their item to the exchange when a prospective buyer is located. The item is inspected, then shipped to the interested party. Upon the buyer's acceptance, the exchange pays the seller.

- **Business History:** Collectors' Marketplace's newsletter/listing "Catalog" is mailed nationwide, which permits the seller to receive the broadest possible exposure. For the buyer, this firm's service ensures that an item is thoroughly checked for condition and authenticity. Their 20-24 page monthly newsletter keeps subscribers aware of current asking prices, market trends and general news in the secondary marketplace. Annual subscription is $20.

Collectors Plates

7308 Izard St.
Omaha, NE 68114
Phone: 402/391-3469

- **Store Hours:** Daily: 1:00-10:00p.m. - by appointment.

- **Secondary Market Lines:** Bradford plates, Royal Copenhagen, Bing & Grondahl, P. Buckley Moss plates, Perillo, M.I. Hummel, Duncan Royale, Lilliput Lane, Hamilton and Ashton-Drake dolls.

  Secondary Market Terms: Buy outright. Consignments. Call for details.

- **Business History:** Collectors since 1952, Ross and Ruth Ernst started a mail order buisness in 1969, selling plates and eventually figurines. Daughter, Ruth Ann, joined the family business several years later and is a very knowledgeable addition to the operation.

  Plates and Hummels are this firm's specialty. The Ernst family does insurance appraisals in both areas. The company buys entire collections and estates and makes these items available to collectors. Prices quoted upon request.

  Collectors Plates is an authorized Redemption Center for Perillo, Duncan Royale and Lilliput Lane collector clubs.

• • • • • • •

Collectors Unlimited

2164 Argentine Road
Howell, MI 48843
Phone: 517/548-0564
Phone: 517/546-1459

- **Store Hours:** By appointment only. Will ship.

- **Secondary Market Lines:** Very large Emmett Kelly, Jr. collection(plates, figurines, ornaments), Lowell Davis (plates, figurines, ornaments), Duncan Royale, Whitley Bay, large inventory of Rockwell plates, figurines and ornaments, Precious Moments, Hibel dolls and plates, Dolls by Jerri, Lilliput Lane, Maud Humphrey, Krystonia, David Winter, Ashton-Drake dolls, Tom Clark Gnomes, Goebel.

- **Secondary Market Terms:** Consignments. Buy outright.

- **Business History:** A relatively new business venture for Jan Bidwell and Joe McCoy, both have been collectors of antiques and collectibles for many years. Collectors Unlimited is a Redemption Center for Dolls by Jerri, Duncan Royale and Lowell Davis. Appraisals are available for collectors seeking to insure their collectibles. Call for details.

• • • • • • •

Collector's World

2249 Honolulu Ave.
Montrose, CA 91020
Phone: 818/248-9451
Fax: 818/248-0439

DISCOVER

- **Store Hours:** Monday–Saturday: 10:00-5:30.

- **Secondary Market Lines:** All God's Children, Chilmark, David Winter, DeGrazia, Jan Hagara, M.I. Hummel, Thomas Kinkade, Legends Pewter, Lilliput Lane, Lladro, Lowell Davis, Maud Humphrey, Memories of Yesterday, Robert Olszewski, Swarovski, Tom Clark Gnomes, Wee Forest Folk.

- **Secondary Market Terms:** Limited Consignments. Buy outright. Call for details.

- **Business History:** Collector's World has over 17 years of experience in servicing both novice and experienced collectors alike in obtaining hard-to-find retired, discontinued or limited production items. They stock a large inventory of secondary market items in their normal lines and have worldwide connections in locating specific items. They maintain their own large active "want" to buy and sell computerized collector listings.

Colonial House Antiques

182 Front St.
Berea, OH 44017
Phone: 800/344-9299
Fax: 216/826-0839

- **Store Hours:** Monday–Saturday: 10:00-5:00.

- **Secondary Market Lines:** Royal Doulton, M.I.
  Hummel, David Winter, Department 56: Snow Village, Dickens
  Village, Christmas in the City, New England, Snowbabies;
  Lilliput Lane, Duncan Royale, Wee Forest Folk, Precious
  Moments, Lladro, Maurice Wideman

- **Secondary Market Terms:** No consignments. Buy
  outright. Layaway available.

- **Business History:** Colonial House Antiques is located in a
  century house in a southwest suburb of Cleveland, Ohio. The store
  features twelve rooms of collectibles and antiques, covering two
  floors. They opened a Christmas store within their existing structure
  in August 1992, featuring an excellent selection of holiday collectibles.

  Colonial House redeems collector club pieces for all lines carried
  and has an appraisal service available. Stan Worry, proprietor, has
  been in the collectible business for over 17 years.

• • • • • • •

Cooper's Jewelry Ltd.

303 W. State St.
Sycamore, IL 60178
Phone: 815/895-3377

- **Store Hours:** Monday, Wednesday, Thursday: 9:00-5:30. Friday: 9:00-8:30. Saturday: 9:00-4:00. Tuesday: Answering machine.

- **Secondary Market Lines:** Christmas ornaments: Gorham, Lunt, Kirk-Stieff, Reed & Barton, Sculpture Design Workshop, Towle, Wallace. Figurines: Authorized M.I. Hummel dealer.

- **Secondary Market Terms:** Generally buy outright. Call for details.

- **Business History:** As a jewelry store, Cooper's has been in business 39 years, and in the collectible ornament business since the first issuance of the 1970 Gorham Snowflake. They have seen ornament collecting grow from the interest of a few, to one of America's favorite hobbies. They specialize in the collectible ornament mail order business and publish informational catalogs twice a year upon request. The store makes a great effort to supply what customers are seeking. They enjoy their business and take pride, in providing friendly, enthusiastic and knowledgeable service to their customers!

Village Realty/
"The Cottage Collector"

6211 Oakmont Blvd. #381
Fort Worth, TX 76132
Phone: 817/294-1961
Phone: 800/874-0126 (Orders)

Village Realty...
...*Miniature Collectible Properties*

- **Hours:** Monday–Friday: 9:00-4:30.

- **Secondary Market Lines:** Department 56, Lilliput Lane, David Winter, and all other cottage lines.

- **Secondary Market Terms:** Buy/sell brokerage. 25% commission added to seller's asking price. Full price is always quoted. Call for details.

- **Business History:** In an effort to complete her Department 56 collection, Patricia M. Cantrell ran an ad to locate the remaining pieces -- and was swamped by calls from collectors who were looking for those same pieces and more. That was all that was needed for the retired antique dealer to re-enter the business world in 1989 and begin a thriving secondary market publication, aimed at educating collectors about their hobby and giving them an opportunity to buy and sell their "real estate!"

  "The Cottage Collector" is a lovely glossy 28-page newsletter, generously sprinkled with photographs. The publication is available six times annually, and subscriptions run $24.00 per year. Subscribers may list the availability of their cottages with the "Village Realty," and several pages of current listings are included in each issue. Orders are placed by calling the firm's 800 number.

• • • • • • •

Cottage Garden

2368 Ingleside Avenue
Macon, GA 31204
Phone: 912/743-9897
Phone: 800/800-1559

- **Store Hours:** Monday–Friday: 10:00-5:30. Saturday: 10:00-5:00.

- **Secondary Market Lines:** Lilliput Lane, Lowell Davis, Wee Forest Folk, Maud Humphrey, Bradford Plates, David Winter, LEGENDS, Hamilton plates, Dave Grossman. Open to other lines.

- **Secondary Market Terms:** Locator and listing service. Layaways. Free shipping on orders over $100.

- **Business History:** Husband and wife team, Jeanette and Steve Wall, have collected Bradford plates since 1977. In 1989, they purchased a local gift shop and immediately started adding additional collectible lines. They now offer over thirty lines and continue to search for promising new lines. The Walls take a personal interest in learning about artists and new lines as they are introduced, and then sharing this information with their customers. Customer service is their top priority. A member of NALED, the Cottage Garden is a Redemption Center for Lilliput Lane, Lowell Davis, Maud Humphrey, All God's Children, Sarah's Attic, Memories of Yesterday, David Winter, Sandra Kuck, Duncan Royale, Marty Bell, Jan Hagara, Iris Arc and LEGENDS. The Walls publish a quarterly newsletter, which is complimentary to all their customers. This publication includes information on new introductions, backstamps, artist signings, awards, retirement announcements and their in-store collectors club.

• • • • • • •

The Cottage Locator

211 North Bridebrook Road
East Lyme, CT 06333
Phone: 203/739-0705   𝔗𝔥𝔢 𝔠𝔬𝔱𝔱𝔞𝔤𝔢 𝔏𝔬𝔠𝔞𝔱𝔬𝔯

- **Exchange Hours:** Open 9:00-5:00, plus 24-hour answering service. Call anytime and calls will be returned the same day

- **Secondary Market Lines:** Department 56: All Villages and accessories, Snowbabies,Waterglobes, music boxes, Department 56 ornaments, including cold cast porcelains.

- **Secondary Market Terms:** Buy/sell brokerage. 20% commission.

- **Business History:** As collectors of Department 56 villages and related items since 1986, Frank and Florence Wilson have watched the phenomenal growth and interest exhibited by collectors who wish to obtain the retired and limited edition pieces. The Cottage Locator was established in 1991, in response to the growing demand by collectors who seek retired Department 56 pieces. This firm is an excellent secondary buy/sell/trade source, having contacts nationwide.

  In addition to listing pieces on the exchange, The Cottage Locator will list trades and keep a record of pieces that collectors are looking for and notify these Department 56 enthusiasts as these items become available. For more information, call for details. The Wilsons also assist collectors with appraisals for insurance purposes and attend and exhibit at retail open houses, where they also speak on many topics.

• • • • • • •

Cottage Park

P.O. Box 411
Greendale, WI 53129
Phone: 414/421-8877

- **Store Hours:** Monday–Friday: 8:30-4:00.

- **Secondary Market Lines:** David Winter, Malcolm Cooper pubs, Lilliput Lane.

- **Secondary Market Terms:** No consignments. Buy outright.

- **Business History:** In 1980, Dick Maslowski entered the giftware business when he purchased two Wicks 'n' Sticks stores, one in Greendale and the other in Madison. His two stores were the first Wicks 'n' Sticks to carry David Winter cottages and Malcolm Cooper pubs. The stores are also Redemption Centers for David Winter and Lilliput Lane collector clubs. Today, these establishments host in-store events, including artist appearances to promote the collectibles hobby.

  Cottage Park was started in 1985, due to the great secondary market demand for collectible cottages. Dick Maslowski offers buyers the opportunity to purchase retired cottages which are also available on layaway. Cottage Park publishes an informative newsletter three times annually, and they are free of charge with a purchase.

Country Charm House

247 West Main Street, Route 23
Leola, PA 17540
Phone: 717/656-7212

- **Store Hours:** Monday–Saturday: 9:30-5:00. Friday: 9:30-9:00.

- **Secondary Market Lines:** June McKenna, Department 56, Maud Humphrey, Jan Hagara, Alex Haley.

- **Secondary Market Terms:** Buy outright. Call for details.

- **Business History:** Country Charm House is a gift shop which opened in 1984 and expanded three years later at its original site. Collectors will enjoy shopping in this charming 100-year-old house, which carries collectibles and the store's own unique floral designs, which constitute a major portion of their business. They also provide home accessorizing services. Other collectible lines include Lizzie High dolls, M.I. Hummel, Zook dolls and Maurice Wideman. They possess a great deal of knowledge about June McKenna, as they have carried June McKenna's early pieces and continue carrying her yearly editions.

  Collectors will appreciate working with the Country Charm House staff, who are dependable and a reliable source in locating new or retired collectibles.

Country Friends

3865 East 82nd St.
Indianapolis, IN 46240
Phone: 317/576-0253

- **Store Hours:** Monday–Saturday: 10:00-6:00. Sunday: 12:00-5:00.

- **Secondary Market Lines:** Department 56: All Villages and accessories.

- **Secondary Market Terms:** Buy outright. Some consignment. Call for details. Buy single pieces or entire collections of retired Heritage Village pieces for cash.

- **Business History:** Country Friends was established in 1985 by the Staffords as a country gift shop. Over the past five years they have more than quadrupled the size of their three stores and developed a reputation for quality country accessories, gifts and furnishings.

  Collectors of Department 56, the Staffords visited a company showroom and decided shortly thereafter to open a store and feature Department 56 collectibles. Today, Country Friends is one of the largest Heritage Village dealers in Indiana, in addition to showcasing other collectibles and gift items.

  Artist appearances are scheduled throughout the year, and secondary market price lists are available at no charge upon request.

• • • • • • •

Crayon Soup

King of Prussia Plaza
King of Prussia, PA 19406
Phone: 215/265-2446
Phone: 215/265-0458

- **Store Hours:** Monday–Saturday: 10:00-9:30. Sunday:
  11:00-5:00.

- **Secondary Market Lines:** All God's Children, Lladro,
  Department 56: Heritage Village and accessories, Snowbabies,
  Lilliput Lane, Emmett Kelly, Jr., David Winter, Precious
  Moments, PenDelfin, Sarah's Attic, Swarovski, Cat's Meow,
  Steinbach Nutcrackers, M.I. Hummel, Memories of Yesterday,
  Maud Humphrey, Norman Rockwell, ANRI, Olszewski
  Miniatures, Anheuser and German Gentz steins.

- **Secondary Market Terms:** Buy outright.

- **Business History:** The formation of Crayon Soup in
  1982 was a natural, considering that owners Joe and Trish
  Zawislack had already been collecting for 20 years! The
  store started in a mall kiosk, with the couple selling stickers
  and novelties geared toward children. Eventually, the
  Zawislacks entered the collectibles market. The name,
  Crayon Soup, was the brainchild of Trish, who formulated
  the name, thinking the couple would start an educational
  store for children! Today, the store is a Redemption Center
  for several collectible lines. Hummel enthusiasts will be
  delighted to view over 700 Hummels in stock. Crayon Soup
  hosts several artist appearances and organizes in-store collector clubs. Information on new and retired products and
  collectors clubs is available free of charge.

Creative Hands

243 R.P. Coffin Road
Long Grove, IL 60047
Phone: 708/634-0545
Phone: 708/459-1922 after 5:00.

CREATIVE HANDS

- **Store Hours:** Daily:10:30-5:00.

- **Secondary Market Lines:** Wee Forest Folk.

- **Secondary Market Terms:** Buy, sell or trade.

- **Business History:** Collectors who enjoy the endearing miniature figurines sculpted by Annette Peterson of Wee Forest Folk will be captivated by the Wee Forest Folk museum at Creative Hands. The museum contains most of the retired pieces. This store is one of Wee Forest Folk's oldest and largest accounts, selling the line since 1978. They generally have 150-200 retired pieces for sale on any given day.

  Creative Hands also offers appraisals of collections and restoration of damaged pieces.

• • • • • • •

Curio Cabinet & Christmas Village

679 High St.
Worthington, OH 43085
Phone: 614/885-1986
Fax: 614/885-2043

Curio Cabinet of Olde Worthington
Distinctive Gifts & Collectibles
and
Christmas Village

- **Store Hours:** Monday–Saturday: 10:00-5:30. Friday 10:00-9:00. Extended Seasonal Hours.

- **Secondary Market Lines:** Wee Forest Folk, Department 56, Maud Humphrey, Royal Doulton, David Winter, All God's Children, Duncan Royale, Lilliput Lane, Olszewski miniatures.

- **Secondary Market Terms:** No consignments. Buy outright. Call for details.

- **Business History:** The Curio Cabinet has expanded greatly since its inception in 1985. What started out as a small collectibles store specializing in Royal Doulton figurines and jugs, has now become a large collectibles store specializing in a wide variety of items including most secondary markets.

  This year, Nicki and Al Budin opened an annex to their store in Worthington called Christmas Village. This store specializes in Christmas collectibles such as June McKenna, Snowbabies, Constance Collection, Duncan Royale and other Christmas collectible items. Nicki has also been doing appraisals for Royal Doulton for several years. She was instrumental in helping write *The Official Royal DoultonPrice Guide* by Ruth Pollard.

• • • • • • •

Cuties Bears & Stuffies

1387 Fall River Ave., Rt.6
Seekonk, Mass. 02771
Phone: 508/336-7868

- **Store Hours:** Tuesday– Saturday: 10:00-5:30. Sunday:
  12:00-4:00. Closed Sundays in June, July and August.

- **Secondary Market Lines:** Daddy Longlegs, All God's
  Children, Miss Martha's Originals, Bette Ball, Madame
  Alexander, Precious Moments, Possible Dreams, Franklin Mint
  dolls, Mattel, Himstedt, Barbie. Check for other doll lines.
  Plates: Bradford, Hamilton, Reco, Artaffects, Maud Humphrey.

- **Secondary Market Terms:** Consignments. Buy outright. Call for details.

- **Business History:** Maria Ferris has been active on the secondary market for 28 years, specializing in antiques, dolls and teddy
  bears. Her son, Barry, joined the business ten years ago. Maria and
  Barry enjoy the challenge of seeking hard-to-find retired collectibles.

  Located near Newport and Providence, Cuties Bears & Stuffies
  offers collectors a wide range of opportunities. The shop hosts an in-
  store collectors club. Interested individuals should write for details.
  Flyers and newsletters, mailed regularly, feature the latest primary
  and secondary market news and consignment information. Annual
  open houses are hosted by the shop. Large groups may also make a
  special appointment with the store for their own store tour and special event.

• • • • • • •

D & A Investments

2055 Burnside Circle
Salt Lake City, UT 84109
Phone: 801/277-4767

- **Store Hours:** Monday–Friday: 9:00-6:00.

- **Secondary Market Lines:** American Breweriana
  Products: Budweiser, Coors, Miller, Stroh's, Heileman,
  Hamm's; Mugs and Steins, Collector Plates, Christmas
  Ornaments.

- **Secondary Market Terms:** No consignments. Buy
  outright. Will purchase complete collections. Call for latest
  price list and for more details. Photos available.

- **Business History:** D & A Investments started as a hobby in
  1985. Due to the great demand in Breweriana collectibles, they soon
  became a full time business, offering other collectors new and hard-
  to-find products. This business also covers the secondary market for
  replica brewery vintage vehicles, neons, lighted signs, mirrors,
  clocks and more. Now, they are one of the Western states' largest
  dealers with over 15,000 items in inventory.

  Their networking system with other dealers can help locate items
  they don't have in stock or put the collector in direct contact with the
  dealer. They have a complete showroom shop for the collector,
  although their main distribution of product is mail order.

  D & A backs every item of merchandise with their 100% money-
  back 30-day time limit guarantee.

• • • • • • •

Darle's Dolls & Bears

1185 Sagamore Parkway West
West Lafayette, IN 47906
Phone: 317/497-0303
Phone: 317/463-1340

- **Store Hours:** Monday–Saturday: 10:00-5:30.

- **Secondary Market Lines:** Dolls: Middleton, Hamilton
Heritage, Barbie, Himstedt, Robin Woods, Bradley, Sandra
Kuck, Effanbee, Madame Alexander; Jan Hagara, Maud
Humphrey, Lowell Davis, V.F. Fine Arts.

- **Secondary Market Terms:** Consignments. Buy outright. Layaway program.

- **Business History:** A collector since childhood, owner
Darle Griffith began her store in 1982, although she became
active in the secondary market in 1980. Darle's Dolls & Bears
is one of the largest doll stores in the area, hosting open
houses, special events and promotions throughout the year.

Darle Griffith is considered an authority in the doll field. She
is a member of the United Federation of Doll Collectors
(NFDC) and is a past president of the local chapter. Darle
speaks to local organizations on the subject of dolls and
bears.

Darle's Dolls & Bears is an excellent source for locating
retired dolls and figurines. Call for details.

The Diamond Connection

6740 E. Ten Mile Road
Centerline, MI 48015
Phone: 313/759-2520

- **Store Hours:** Monday–Friday: 11:00-7:30. Saturday: 10:00-6:00.

- **Secondary Market Lines:** Gartlan USA, Salvino Inc., Sports Impressions.

- **Secondary Market Terms:** Consignments and outright buys are acceptable. Please call for details.

- **Business History:** The Diamond Connection has only been in existence since 1991 as a retail outlet, but its owners Steve Graus, John Moore and Dave Schulte have marketed porcelain sports collectibles for over five years via trade shows and mail order. The Diamond Connection features sports figurines and plates from Gartlan USA, Salvino, Sports Impressions, Pro Sports and DH Ussher Ltd. Product assortment includes lithographs from Pro Art, Sports Collectible Warehouse and artists Doug West and Ed LaPere. The store has featured GartlanUSA's personable artist, Michael J. Taylor for an in-store personal appearance and is a Redemption Center for Gartlan and Sports Impressions Collector Clubs. The Diamond Connection publishes a bimonthly newsletter and is very active in the secondary market. Please call collect with any questions or to be placed on the mailing list.

• • • • • • •

Dickens' Exchange, Inc.

700 Phosphor Ave. Suite A
Metairie, LA 70005
Phone: 504/832-4157

- **Store Hours:** Monday–Friday: 9:00-5:30. Sat.: 10:00-2:00.

- **Secondary Market Lines:** Department 56: Snow Village, Dickens Village, Christmas in the City, New England, Alpine, Little Town of Bethlehem, North Pole, cold cast porcelains, Snowbabies and accessories.

- **Secondary Market Terms:** 10% commission paid by purchaser on consignment listings. Exchange sells outright - no commissions. Call for details.

- **Business History:** Lynda Blankenship began as a collector of Department 56 collectibles. Along the way, she made "long distance" friends with other Department 56 enthusiasts. Lynda enjoyed researching her hobby and before long, became known as an excellent source for information. In January 1990, when it became impossible to speak to each party individually, Lynda began writing letters to her friends. By April of that same year, those initial letters evolved into "The Dickens' Exchange," a reliable source for Department 56 news and a thriving exchange. Today, Lynda publishes a 20-page newsletter which boasts nearly 4,000 subscribers! She describes her newsletter as a place for collectors to meet and share their hobby. Lynda hosts private engagements all over the country, often in conjunction with shows and conventions. She hosts seminars on many topics, and is a member of Prodigy. Collectors created a column for her on this computer network called "Ask Lynda," where she answers collectors' Department 56 related questions.

• • • • • • •

Don's Collectibles

3020 E. Majestic Ridge
Las Cruces, NM 88001
Phone: 505/522-3721
Phone: 800/827-3721
Fax: 505/646-5421

Don's Collectibles

- **Store Hours:** By appointment.

- **Secondary Market Lines:** Bossons, M.I.Hummel.

- **Secondary Market Terms:** Buy, sell, trade and restore. Call or write for details. No consignments. Cash paid for discontinued Bossons, Fraser-Art (Division W.H. Bossons - Sales - Ltd., Congleton, England); and Crown, Full Bee and Stylized Bee markings of M.I. Hummel Artware, products of W. Goebel Porzellanfabrik, Roedental, Germany. 100% guaranteed satisfaction for all sales and restoration work with sales quotations and work estimates provided free of charge.

- **Business History:** Don's Collectibles is primarily a mail order business. Dr. Donald M. Hardisty, owner, is a full time music professor at New Mexico State University, and became interested in Bossons artware about 20 years ago. He and his wife, Barbara, are members of the M.I. Hummel Club, and Charter and Life Members of the International Bossons Collectors Society. Don is a recognized Bossons restoration artist, approved by Bossons. The discontinued Bossons can be worth $85 and up, with a few rare Bossons valued at over $10,000. Don's artistic repairs of Bossons artware, fine porcelain and Hummel figurines have been widely acclaimed. References furnished upon request.

• • • • • • •

Doris' Collectibles

P.O. Box 183 183 Main Street
St. Peter, IL 62880
Phone: 618/349-8780
Phone: 800/289-4042
Fax: 618/349-6245

- **Store Hours:** Monday–Friday: 9:00-5:00. Other times by appointment.

- **Secondary Market Lines:** Gartlan, Salvino, Sports Impressions, Precious Moments, M.I. Hummel, Gone With the Wind collectibles, Sports Memorabilia, Bradford, Hamilton and other plates, specializing in sports collectible magazines.

- **Secondary Market Terms:** Some consignment. Buy outright. Buy/sell brokerage. Call for details.

- **Business History:** Doris' Collectibles is a family owned and operated business, established in 1976 by Doris and Elmer Wollin. A NALED member, Doris' Collectibles is a moderately sized store in a small town with a grand vision of serving the collector through its mail order business and show attendance. The store is a Redemption Center for Precious Moments, Gartlan USA, Salvino and M.I. Hummel. Doris' Collectibles is considered a secondary market specialist in sports collectibles, including various collectible publications. Doris' has numerous hard to find back issues of the *Legends Sports Memorabilia, Cartwright's Journal of Baseball Collectibles* and *Investor's Journal* . They also feature new editions from today's growing field of sports collectible magazines. Collectors are invited to call or send for a complimentary issue of Mark's newsletter, dealing with sports news and collectibles.

Eilene's Treasures

P.O. Box 285
285 Sunset Drive
Virden, IL 62690
Phone: 217/965-3648

- **Store Hours:** Daily: 8:00-8:00. If no answer, please leave message on machine. Calls will be returned within 24 hours.

- **Secondary Market Lines:** Precious Moments, suspended and retired: figurines, bells, ornaments, plates; Memories of Yesterday figurines and ornaments, Hallmark Ornaments, Enesco Treasury Ornaments.

- **Secondary Market Terms:** Buy outright. Layaways available. Fair prices. Satisfaction guaranteed.

- **Business History:** Eilene's Treasures is a secondary market mail order business which had a unique beginning. In 1984, Eilene Kruse and her husband owned a car dealership. A young woman who owned a beautiful Precious Moments collection offered it to Eilene who was, herself, a Precious Moments collector. She agreed to purchase it and retained most of the collection, while selling the remaining pieces. That was the beginning of the end.

  Today, Eilene Kruse is an expert on Precious Moments marks, as she purchased many early pieces with original marks. She then expanded her business to include other Enesco lines and Hallmark ornaments. Eilene attends four to five ornament and collectibles shows in the Illinois area and publishes a price list which is available upon request.

• • • • • • •

Ellis In Wonderland

2533 Fair Oaks Blvd.
Sacramento CA 95825
Phone: 916/485-2295

- **Store Hours:** Monday–Friday: 10:00-6:00. Saturday: 11:00-6:00, Sunday: 12:00-3:00.

- **Secondary Market Lines:** Chilmark, Lladro, Swarovski, David Winter, Lilliput Lane, Legends, Polland Studios, Michael Boyett Studio, Caithness, Armani.

- **Secondary Market Terms:** Buy outright. Buy/sell listings with 20% of selling price commission upon completion of sale.

- **Business History:** Established in 1980, Ellis in Wonderland specializes in fine collectibles. They are a full service redemption center for lines listed above and feature periodic artist appearances and other in-store events. Owner, Sandie Ellis, is a member of the Chilmark Advisory Council and Miniature Sculpture Association Advisory Board.

Eloise's Gifts & Antiques

722 South Goliad
Rockwall, TX 75087
Phone: 214/771-6371

- **Store Hours:** Monday–Saturday: 10:00-6:00. Sunday: 12:00-6:00.

- **Secondary Market Lines:** Department 56: Heritage Village; Tom Clark, Lowell Davis, Frumps, Ray Day, M.I. Hummel, Jan Hagara, Sarah's Attic, Pocket Dragons, David Winter, All God's Children, Duncan Royale, Emmett Kelly, Jr., Windy Meadows, Maud Humphrey.

- **Secondary Market Terms:** Trades. Buy outright or consignment, depending on the present inventory. Three month layaway. All items will be listed on a secondary market computer program to match buyers and sellers.

- **Business History:** Eloise's Gifts and Antiques was founded by Eloise Cullum and her partner Ethel Moss. It has grown from a gift shop/tearoom to a large collectible center, now owned by the original partners and Sue Reeves. Eloise's serves the Dallas metroplex and carries extensive current inventory in the lines listed above. They also are Bradford/NALED members and carry Goebel Miniatures, Lladro, Lilliput Lane, Melody in Motion, Enesco, Sandicast, United Design, Hibel, Swarovski and Wee Forest Folk.

The Emporium

3358 West 26th Street
Erie, PA 16506
Phone: 814/833-2895

- **Store Hours:** Monday-Saturday: 10:00-5:00. Special holiday hours.

- **Secondary Market Lines:** Lowell Davis, Jan Hagara, Krystonia, June McKenna, Sarah's Attic, Ron Lee Clowns.

- **Secondary Market Terms:** Some consignments. Layaways available.

- **Business History:** The Emporium is a restored home, circa 1840, which has been turned into a charming store for all seasons. A typical farmhouse design for the era, it features keyhole doorways, a carved staircase and fieldstone foundations.

  Owner Audrey Theobald opened The Emporium in 1980, featuring the artwork of June McKenna and presently displays one of the largest selections in the country. Today, this store carries unusual gifts for every member of the family, as well as numerous collectible lines including Department 56, The Collectables porcelain dolls, David Winter, Annalee dolls, Ron Lee clowns, Kitty Cucumber, carousel horses by Willetts and PJ's, Lynn Haney Santas and more!

  A member of NALED, The Emporium hosts one or two open houses annually and publishes newsletters, which are available upon request.

• • • • • • •

Estes Silver & Gold

153 Virginia Dr.
P.O. Box 3639
Estes Park, CO 80517
Phone: 303/586-6276

- **Store Hours:** Winter: Daily, 9:00-5:30. Summer: 9:00-9:00.

- **Secondary Market Lines:** All plates, coins, Hummel, Precious Moments, ANRI, DeGrazia, Swarovski, David Winter, Enesco Treasury Ornaments, Memories of Yesterday, Maruri, Daniel Monfort sculptures, most limited edition prints, including but not limited to Redlin, Peterson, Stone, Zolan.

- **Secondary Market Terms:** No consignments. Buy outright.

- **Business History:** In business since 1979, Larry Pierce has accumulated one of the largest plate inventories for back issues in the country, and can assist collectors in locating those that he doesn't already have in stock. This business is very service oriented, shipping worldwide and never canceling a back order. The firm also buys and sells retired figurines and prints. In fact, they actively seek to buy large collections and invite collectors to call for more information. Estes Silver & Gold is a Redemption Center for M.I. Hummel, Precious Moments, Duncan Royale, Perillo, Sandra Kuck and David Winter collector clubs.

  Since 1987, an additional store operating under the name Glenwood Fine Gifts and Coins has been servicing the collector in Glenwood Springs, Colorado near Aspen.

• • **76** • •

• • • • • • •

Eureka! Collectibles

P.O. Box 212
Merrick, NY 11566
Phone: 516/889-8808
Phone: 516/897-7338
Fax: 516/897-7338 Call before faxing.

- **Hours:** Monday–Friday: 5:00pm-9:00. Saturday & Sunday: 12:00-5:00pm. Answering service available 10:00am-5:00pm.

- **Secondary Market Lines:** Swarovski, David Winter, Lilliput Lane, Precious Moments, M.I. Hummel: Century pieces, clubs, plates, bells; Department 56: Snow Village, Dickens, Christmas in the City and accessories; Goebel Miniatures, De Grazia: mini plates, and more; Royal Doulton, and new lines always being added.

- **Secondary Market Terms:** Buy/sell and brokerage. Call for details.

- **Business History:** Formerly of Jamens Collectibles, one of the largest collectibles dealers on the east coast, the owners decided to concentrate their efforts on the ever-expanding secondary market and recently formed Eureka! Collectibles. This business specializes in the aftermarket for Goebel Miniatures, David Winter and Royal Doulton as well as many other lines. Eureka! provides price lists for these lines and more. They keep collectors' 'want' items on their list for three months. They also enjoy doing searches for any collectible and will do appraisals for insurance purposes. Collectors are invited to contact Eureka! for details on any of these services. Eureka! Collectibles will continue their ten year tradition of traveling around the country, attending secondary market shows.

• • • • • • •

European Imports & Gifts

Oak Mill Mall, 7900 North Milwaukee
Niles, IL 60648
Phone: 708/967-5253 (IL); 800/227-8670
Fax: 708/967-0133

- **Store Hours:** Monday-Friday: 10:00 to 8:00. Saturday: 10:00-5:30. Sunday: 12:00-5:00. Nov. 1-Dec.26: Mon.-Fri: 10:00-9:00.

- **Secondary Market Lines:** Annalee, ANRI, Armani, Artaffects, Ashton-Drake, Bradford plates, Maud Humphrey, Byers' Choice, Cairn Gnomes, Chilmark, Lowell Davis, Department 56 including Snowbabies, Duncan Royale, Goebel Miniatures, Gorham dolls, Jan Hagara, Hamilton dolls and plates, Lizzie High, M.I. Hummel, Kaiser, Emmett Kelly, Jr., Krystonia, Sandra Kuck, Legends, Lenox, Lilliput Lane, Lladro, Memories of Yesterday, All God's Children, Norman Rockwell, Precious Moments, Royale Doulton, Sandicast, Sebastian Miniatures, Sports Impressions, Steiff, Swarovski, Enesco's Treasury of Christmas Ornaments, United Design, WACO, Wee Forest Folk, Maurice Wideman, David Winter, Whitley Bay.

- **Secondary Market Terms:** No consignments. Buy outright: mail a complete listing. Call for details.

- **Business History:** European Imports is an established secondary market retailer. Since 1967, European Imports' range of collectibles has grown from a few M. I. Hummels to one of the largest collectible showcases in the United States. European Imports is a member of NALED, and owner Edward W. Delgau serves on advisory boards for many of today's top collectible firms. The shop carries most secondary market price guides and ships free anywhere in the continental U.S. for purchases over $50.00.

• • • • • • •

Eva Marie, Dry Grocer

1915 S. Catalina Ave.
Redondo Beach, CA 90277
Phone: 310/375-8422

- **Store Hours:** Monday–Saturday: 10:00-6:00.

- **Secondary Market Lines:** Precious Moments, M.I. Hummel, All God's Children, Lowell Davis, Tom Clark, David Winter, Memories of Yesterday. Large plate inventory secondary source for closed issues.

- **Secondary Market Terms:** Cash, check or credit card. Layaway available. Ship UPS daily.

- **Business History:** Eva Marie Dry Grocer sells primary and secondary market lines. In 1990, 1991 and 1992, The Bradford Exchange presented Eva Marie an award at the South Bend show for being a top seller of secondary plates in the United States. The store has two thousand plates on display. They are hung on a display board, like a book hung on the wall. Collectors can stand in one spot and move the boards to view and compare the work of many artists.

Eva Marie is a member of The Bradford Exchange and the National Association of Limited Edition Dealers. The store is a Redemption Center for many collector clubs.

Collectors who want to learn more about collecting limited editions are invited to contact Eva Marie.

Eve's Collectors' Show

P.O. Box 25024
Fort Wayne, IN 46825-0024
Phone: 219/637-5708

- **Office Hours:** Show information: Monday–Friday: 9:00-5:00. 24 hour answering service. Show hours: 9:00-3:00.

- **Secondary Market Lines:** Available at Eve's shows: Hallmark, Precious Moments, Department 56, Memories of Yesterday, Enesco, Carlton, David Winter, Lowell Davis, ANRI, Emmett Kelly, Jr., Maud Humphrey, Lladro, Jan Hagara. Some collectibles are available in limited quantities, so call before coming.

- **Secondary Market Terms:** Exhibitors' terms: buy, sell and some trades.

- **Business History:** Eve Baker opened Eve's Books in 1976, but became interested in collectibles when she began collecting in 1985. She sold a few pieces on the secondary market and discovered a need for buyers and sellers to have a place to meet. She then formed Eve's Collectors' Show in 1989, and became a show promoter, while still maintaining her book store!. Today, Eve organizes shows in Fort Wayne, Indiana, Columbus, Ohio and Detroit, Michigan, near Dearborn. Collectors who are interested in purchasing retired collectibles will enjoy attending one of Eve's shows. For a small admission, collectors can view the exhibition hall for an entire day and have a chance to win a door prize, with drawings every hour. Eve's motto is "Today's Collectibles, Tomorrow's Treasures." Collectors interested in obtaining more information about these collectible shows should contact this firm to be placed on the mailing list.

• • • • • • •

Evets Collectibles

5254 NW 94th Doral Place
Miami, FL 33178
Phone: 305/592-5701

- **Store Hours:** By appointment only. Has 24-hour answering machine.

- **Secondary Market Lines:** Beer steins and mugs: Budweiser, Millers, Strohs, Avon, Coors, C.U.I. and many more.

- **Secondary Market Terms:** Buy outright. Call for details.

- **Business History:** An active collector for over ten years, Stephen M. Suhre maintains a showroom featuring over 250 steins and mugs. Make an appointment to view this collection, or send a large self-addressed stamped envelope for a price list. Evets Collectibles operates a mail order service, in addition to attending antique and collectible shows throughout the country. This firm is a member of the National Association of Breweriana Advertising (NABA) and the American Breweriana Association (ABA).

• • • • • • •

Expressions Collectibles, Inc.

7950 E. Acoma Dr. Ste. 100
Scottsdale, AZ 85260
Phone: 602/443-3074

- **Store Hours:** Home Office: Monday–Friday: 8:30-4:00.

- **Secondary Market Lines:** Chilmark, Lilliput Lane, Department 56 including Snowbabies, Lladro, M.I. Hummel, Precious Moments, Goebel Miniatures, David Winter, German Nutcrackers, Armani, Ron Lee Clowns, Maruri.

- **Secondary Market Terms:** Buy outright. Call for details.

- **Business History:** Expressions Collectibles, Inc. is one of the West's largest collectible dealers. Ken Gallagher has served on the Advisory Council of the Lance Corporation for several years and is one of the country's foremost experts on pewter sculptures. With the opening of Gallagher's in the Scottsdale Galleria in the spring of 1991, Expressions Collectibles, Inc. established one of the largest collections of retired collectible figurines and sculptures open for the public in the country. Mr. Gallagher has served as an appraiser expert and advisor to many insurance companies on matters relating to collectibles.

  Store locations: Phoenix: Paradise Valley Mall (602) 996-8610, Metrocenter Mall (602) 943-6816, Westridge Mall (602) 272-4840; Scottsdale: Scottsdale Galleria (602) 970-0801; Mesa: Superstition Springs Mall (602) 641-0913; Tucson: Tucson Mall (602) 293-4303; Flagstaff: Flagstaff Mall (602) 526-1194.

• • • • • • •

FACET Collector's Showcase

268 Bellevue Sq.
Bellevue, WA 98004
Phone: 800/285-9876
Phone: 206/451-3580

- **Store Hours:** Monday–Saturday: 10:00-9:30, Sunday: 11:00-6:00.

- **Secondary Market Lines:** Lladro, Swarovski, Legends, Chilmark, Hummel, Lilliput Lane, Caithness, Flambro, Royal Doulton, Armani, Ron Lee, Goebel Miniatures.

- **Secondary Market Terms:** Commission market exchange. Possible consignment. Over 20,000 collectors on their mailing list!

- **Business History:** Facet Collector's Showcase is a very attractive collector store specializing in twenty-one of the top collectibles lines. Because of their total focus on these lines and their huge inventory, they offer excellent service to the collector!

  Facet has over 1,000 pieces each of Lladro and Swarovski in stock. They also maintain an inventory of nearly every piece of Chilmark and Legends, in addition to several hundred Lilliput Lane cottages.

  Their 800 number and informed collector staff make it easy to fulfill collectors' needs.

• • • • • •

Figurine World

Lakeforest Mall
701 Russell Ave.
Gaithersburg, MD 20877
Phone: 301/977-3997
Phone: 800/688-5765

- **Store Hours:** Monday–Saturday 10:00-9:30. Sunday: 12:00-6:00.

- **Secondary Market Lines:** Dept. 56, Precious Moments, Tom Clark Gnomes, Goebel Miniatures, M.I. Hummel, Emmett Kelly-Flambro, David Winter Cottages, Lilliput Lane, Swarovski, Sarah's Attic, All God's Children, Lowell Davis, Lladro, Krystonia, Ashton-Drake Dolls, Plates.

- **Secondary Market Terms:** No consignments. Specialize in locating secondary market items from other dealers throughout the United States.

- **Business History:** Carefree Gifts (Figurine World) was established in 1973 by Elizabeth Anders, the first of three generations. At that time, Carefree Gifts was mainly a Hummel mail order business. In 1983, Mrs. Anders, along with her daughter, Judy Koch, and granddaughter, Tammy Kirby, opened a full service collectible store in Lakeforest Mall in Gaithersburg, Maryland. It is known today as Figurine World. In 1986, because of its growth and potential, the store was moved to a much larger location in the same mall. In 1988, Mrs. Anders retired, and Don Argabright became the new partner.

  Today, Figurine World has a marvelous variety of collectible lines from around the world. These include Germany, Spain, Austria, Sweden, Japan and Mexico.

Flash Collectibles

560 N. Moorpark Road Suite 287
Thousand Oaks, CA 91360
Phone: 805/499-9222

FLASH

- **Office Hours:** Tuesday–Saturday: 10:00-5:00 or by chance.
24-hour answering service available.

- **Secondary Market Lines:** Budweiser, Anheuser-Busch, Strohs, Old Style, Miller, Hamms, Pabst, Coors.

- **Secondary Market Terms:** Buy outright.
Consignment and trades. Search service available.
Layaways.

- **Business History:** Flash Collectibles started as a part time business in 1971. By 1973, they were totally consumed by the antique and collectibles "bug" and opened their first store called The Antique Co. This shop carried a mix of furniture and advertising items.

In 1984, Doug and Natalie Marks discovered the Anheuser-Busch collectible steins. They were instantly attracted to their beauty and detail.

In 1986, the firm opened at their current location and changed their name to Flash Collectibles. They specialize in mail order beer steins. They have a free brochure listing their current stock. Call to be added to their mailing list. They also feature movie stills, and an exceptionally large collection of original full-color citrus, apple and vegetable labels.

Fox's Gifts & Collectables

7030 5th Avenue
Scottsdale, AZ 85251
Phone: 602/947-0560
Phone: 800/592-2555

- **Store Hours:** Monday–Saturday: 10:00-5:00.

- **Secondary Market Lines:** DeGrazia, Tom Clark Gnomes, Bing & Grondahl/Royal Copenhagen plates, M.I. Hummel, Department 56: Heritage Village; ANRI, Bradford dealer plates, Hibel, Moss, Fred Stone, Jan Hagara.

- **Secondary Market Terms:** Buy outright.

- **Business History:** Fox's Gifts & Collectables was founded in 1970 and is now owned and managed by Genevra Fox. The store, recently relocated, is prettier than ever! A member of NALED, Fox's is also a Redemption Center for any of the lines listed above that have collector clubs, as well as Lladro, ANRI, Duncan Royale, Chilmark, Sandra Kuck, Maud Humphrey, Precious Moments and Lowell Davis. Collectors will enjoy Fox's complete line of DeGrazia collectibles, past and present, as well as a captivating display of Delftware. Genevra and her staff will answer collectors' questions and search for retired pieces in both lines and other hard-to-find artwork. The highlight of each year at Fox's is the week-long open house, where special events are planned daily. Activities include artist appearances, special sales, the introduction of new DeGrazia pieces and collector club meetings. Fox's publishes a newsletter on plates and figurines and a quarterly DeGrazia newsletter. Collectors may call to be placed on either mailing list.

The Frame Gallery

305 Third Avenue
Chula Vista, CA 91910
Phone: 619/422-1700

- **Store Hours:** Monday–Friday: 10:00-5:30. Saturday: 10:00-5:00.

- **Secondary Market Lines:** All collector plates and prints. Department 56, sports collectibles, Perillo.

- **Secondary Market Terms:** Very flexible. Specializes in searching for hard-to-find collectibles. Does not buy outright. Call for details.

- **Business History:** The Frame Gallery began as a framing shop, but soon, collectors began coming to the store for advice on the art of framing different collectibles. Before long, mother and daughter team, Margaret and Jan introduced collectibles to their store. Today, they are a Redemption Center for Marty Bell, Thomas Kinkade, Memories of Yesterday, Maud Humphrey, Perillo, Miss Martha's Originals and Lilliput Lane. They also carry artists' work of local scenes-- of particular interest to tourists.

  The Frame Gallery welcomes all requests for secondary market pieces. They will spend whatever time is necessary to seek the piece a collector has requested. They have access to avenues for most every line. They truly enjoy the thrill of the hunt!

• • • • • • •

Front Parlor Gift Shop

300 Cemetary Road
Oakland, IL 61943
Phone: 217/346-3533

- **Store Hours:** Daily: 8:00-6:00.

- **Secondary Market Lines:** John Hine Studios: David Winter, Maurice Wideman, Christopher Lawrence Mushrooms, Malcolm Cooper Pubs.

- **Secondary Market Terms:** Buy outright.

- **Business History:** Bette Page, owner of the Front Parlor Gift Shop, has been active in the collectibles business for over 40 years. She presently limits her secondary market exclusively to John Hine collectibles. She has handled David Winter cottages since they were first introduced in 1986 and is a Redemption Center for the club. Bette is also a member of the John Hine Advisory Board.

  Recognized as one of the leading authorities of the David Winter secondary market, Bette has one of the largest inventories of retired cottages anywhere. She ships worldwide at no cost. The Front Parlor invites collectors to join its in-store John Hine collectors club or to send for its price list and store newsletters. Bette offers free appraisals of John Hine artwork to her customers.

• • • • • • •

Gallery II

Georgia Antique Center - Shop 13
6624 N.E. Expressway (I-85)
Atlanta, GA 30093
Phone: 404/872-7272

Mailing Address:
P.O. Box 14244
Atlanta, GA 30324

GALLERY II
For the Discriminating Collector
FIGURINES • COLLECTOR'S PLATES • CLOWNS
DOLLS • LIMITED EDITIONS • COLLECTIBLES

• **Store Hours:** Wednesday–Saturday: 11:00-6:00. Sunday: 12:00-6:00. Phone answered daily: 9:30-5:30.

• **Secondary Market Lines:** Department 56: Dickens Village, New England Village, Christmas in the City, North Pole, Snowbabies; Emmet Kelly, Jr., All God's Children, Royal Doulton, Ashton-Drake dolls, David Winter, Hamilton plates, Duncan Royale, Maud Humphrey, Jan Hagara, Authorized Bradford plate dealer.

• **Secondary Market Terms:** Buy and sell. Ship Worldwide. Layaway. Call for details.

• **Business History:** An avid collector himself, Robert Shulman began his business in 1976. At that time, Gallery II was mainly a mail order business, opening its store in 1979. Today, Gallery II carries over 50 beautiful and diverse lines of collectibles and employs eleven full and part-time associates. Gallery II's staff strives to serve the collector. The store hosts three to six open houses and artist appearances each year. Gallery II also utilizes a computer system with over 250 interest categories that tracks collectors' special interest areas. Customers are then notified when new products are available.

Georgia's Gift Gallery

575 Forest
Plymouth, MI 48170
Phone: 313/453-7733
Phone: 800/562-3655
Fax: 313/453-1596

Georgia's Gift Gallery
Collector Plates • Dolls • Figurines • Lithographs
575 Forest Avenue • Plymouth MI 48170

- **Store Hours:** Monday, Tuesday, Wednesday: 10:00-7:00. Thursday and Friday: 10:00-8:00. Saturday: 10:00-6:00. Sunday: 12:00-5:00.

- **Secondary Market Lines:** Ashton-Drake, Hamilton dolls, Department 56, Lladro, plates, Sandra Kuck graphics.

- **Secondary Market Terms:** No consignments. Buy outright. Layaways available. Free shipping.

- **Business History:** Brother and sister duo, Michael McCarty and Michelle Suttle, opened Georgia's Gift Gallery in 1982 and have developed the business into a top-notch collectibles retail operation aimed at educating and serving the collector. They have been recognized by The Bradford Exchange, having received 22 awards over the years. A member of NALED, this very large store carries a wide variety of collectibles and is a Redemption Center for nearly 30 collector clubs. Georgia's mailing list of 42,000 receives notification of upcoming releases, retirements and open houses. Collectors may call to be placed on the mailing list. Customers who purchase a doll from Georgia's fine selection, receive a complimentary binder entitled "My Doll Diary." Each loose leaf page includes photos and information about Ashton-Drake, Hamilton and Paradise Gallery dolls, in addition to a place to maintain a doll inventory. Updated pages are mailed to collectors as they are published.

The Gift Attic

Crabtree Valley Mall
Raleigh, NC 27612
Phone: 919/781-1822

the Attic

- **Store Hours:** Monday–Saturday: 10:00-9:30.

- **Secondary Market Lines:** Department 56; all Villages, Snowbabies; Tom Clark, Lilliput Lane, David Winter, Miss Martha's Originals, Lowell Davis, Robert Olszewski, ANRI, Duncan Royale, M.I. Hummel, Byers' Choice, Swarovski.

- **Secondary Market Terms:** Call for details.

- **Business History:** Family owned and operated, The Gift Attic was established in 1976. The store is service oriented, with family members and staff each specializing in different collectible lines -- a valuable resource for collectors!

  The Gift Attic is a member of NALED, featuring a full display of each collectible line carried. The store publishes newsletters which are sent to its customer mailing list, and hosts artist appearances and open houses each year. The Gift Attic is a Redemption Center for numerous collector clubs, and in fact, sponsors its own Department 56 club. Interested collectors are invited to call or write for details.

  The Gift Attic staff is willing to seek retired collectible pieces.

Gift Music & Thrift Shoppe

Gift MUSIC MINISTRY

2501 Chicago Rd.
Chicago Heights, IL 60411
Phone: 708/754-4387 - 24 hours

- **Store Hours:** Monday, Wednesday, Friday, Saturday: 10:00-4:00. Tuesday and Thursday: 12:00-7:00. Sunday: "See you in Church."

- **Secondary Market Lines:** Precious Moments and Memories of Yesterday. Locator service for Lladro, M.I. Hummel, All God's Children, David Winter, ANRI, Tom Clark, Department 56, Emmett Kelly, Jr., Lilliput Lane, Hallmark and Enesco ornaments, Rockwell figurines, Fontanini, Remington Bronze, Kurt S. Adler, Midwest Importers and more.

- **Secondary Market Terms:** Consignments. Buy outright. Buy/sell brokerage. Call for information.

- **Business History:** Gift Music Ministry, a not-for-profit traveling religious music group, was begun by Joe and Terri Schulte in 1980. The store is an outgrowth of this ministry and their desire to bring quality religious and inspirational items into more homes. In addition to being active on the secondary market, the store offers an appraisal service. The firm also accepts items and collections for tax-deductible donations. They bring people of various cultures, denominations and backgrounds together to promote understanding and open up new worlds for all concerned.

• • • • • • •

Gifts & Accents

9611 Metcalf Avenue
Overland Park, KS 66212
Phone: 913/381-8856
Phone: 800/822-8856

- **Store Hours:** Monday–Saturday: 10:00-9:00. Sunday: 12:00-5:30.

- **Secondary Market Lines:** Precious Moments. Please call for other lines available during Swap and Sells.

- **Secondary Market Terms:** Consignments: 30% commission.

- **Business History:** In 1980, J.D. Bittel started Gifts & Accents as a gift store in a 2,400 square foot facility, carrying about 20 percent collectibles. Today, the store is 5,000 square feet and carries 80-85 percent collectibles.

  Gifts & Accents is recognized as an authority on Precious Moments, both its primary and secondary markets. They also have connections with many other firms to assist collectors in seeking retired pieces in other lines as well. The store is known for its popular annual Swap and Sells which take place eight days before Mother's Day and the Saturday before Thanksgiving. Typically, a collector can find retired pieces from Precious Moments, Tom Clark Gnomes, Lowell Davis, Jan Hagara, Department 56, M.I. Hummel, David Winter, Lilliput Lane, Lucy Bears, plates, ornaments and more. A member of NALED, Gifts & Accents holds ten to twelve open houses annually and publishes a newsletter.

Gigi's Dolls & Sherry's Teddy Bears, Inc.

7550 N. Milwaukee Ave.
Chicago, IL 60648
Phone: 312/594-1540
Phone: 800/442-3655

*Gigi's Dolls &
Sherry's Teddy Bears, Inc.*

- **Store Hours:** Monday–Saturday: 10:00-5:00. Thursday, Friday: 10:00-9:00. Sunday: 12:00-5:00.

- **Secondary Market Lines:** Lawtons, Ashton-Drake, Annette Himstedt, Effanbee, Barbie, Alexander, Yolanda Bello.

- **Secondary Market Terms:** Buy outright.

- **Business History:** Lifelong doll lovers, Sherry and Gigi entered the business world initially by going to flea markets, house sales and shows. From there, they began exhibiting at various shows locally and then throughout the country, enjoying their business immensely.

  In 1980, Sherry opened a shop in Plainfield, Illinois. Two years later, Gigi made a career change and joined Sherry in the business. The pair moved the store to Oak Mill Mall. In an effort to expand their business, Gigi and Sherry moved to a larger facility in 1991, just five blocks south of Oak Mill Mall.

  This store specializes in dolls, bears, plush, miniatures and dollhouses. Their doll hospital is open January 15 - November 20.

Gingerbread House Gifts & Collectibles

109 S. Miami Street
West Milton, OH 45383
Phone: 513/698-3477
Fax: 513/698-6820

- **Store Hours:** January-October: Tuesday–Saturday: 10:30-5:00. Extended hours and open on Sundays throughout November and December.

- **Secondary Market Lines:** Department 56, Sarah's Attic, Memories of Yesterday, Cat's Meow, Jan Hagara, Lilliput Lane, David Winter.

- **Secondary Market Terms:** Buy/sell brokerage. Buy outright occasionally.

- **Business History:** The Gingerbread House was opened in 1972, but began specializing in collectibles in 1985, when Jerry and Nancy Wahl bought the business.

  The Gingerbread House indeed *looks* like a gingerbread house. It was the *first* house built in the city in 1826! This lovely Victorian home is attractively trimmed in the gingerbread motif.

  The Wahls expanded the original three rooms and one collectible line, to five full rooms and many of today's collectible lines. Collectors will not only enjoy the selection of collectibles, but will also take home a lovely notecard with -- what else -- a delicious gingerbread recipe!

• • • • • •

Glorious Treasures

1865 Flatbush Avenue
Brooklyn, NY 11210
Phone: 718/252-0400
Fax: 718/258-8855

- **Store Hours:** Monday–Saturday: 10:00-6:00.

- **Secondary Market Lines:** Bradford plates, Ashton-Drake dolls, M.I. Hummel, Royal Doulton, Rockwell, Zolan, Kuck, Hibel, Perillo, Francis Hook, Red Skelton, Lowell Davis, Bessie Pease Gutmann, Hagara, Maud Humphrey, DeGrazia, ANRI, Goebel Miniatures, Emmett Kelly, Jr., Disney, Fred Stone, Pat Buckley Moss, Don Polland, John McClelland; Popular culture: Beatles, Elvis, movie stars and movies, music and television; rare coins, bought and sold, and most other collectibles.

- **Secondary Market Terms:** Catalog - price list available. Collectors should state their interest and include a self-addressed, stamped envelope. Items trade and bought as needed. Items taken on consignment at 25% commission plus a $10.00 handling, registration and service charge. Sales by domestic checks, money orders and major credit cards. Discounts of sales transactions subject to method of payment. Sales tax where required and shipping extra.

- **Business History:** Established in 1977, Glorious Treasures is exclusively devoted to limited edition collectibles. The store is an East Coast Redemption Center for the artwork of M.I. Hummel, Sandra Kuck, Gregory Perillo and sports collectibles. Glorious Treasures is also one of the largest authorized specialists, covering the secondary market for old-Bradford plates, as well as an Authorized Bradford Dealer for primary plates at fair prices.

• • • • • • •

GRAHAM'S CRACKERS and Other Collectables

5909 E. 86 Street
Indianapolis, IN 46250
Phone: 317/842-5727

- **Store Hours:** Monday–Saturday: 10:00-9:00. Sunday: 12:00-5:00.

- **Secondary Market Lines:** Department 56: All Villages and Snowbabies; Tom Clark.

- **Secondary Market Terms:** Buy outright, including M.I. Hummel, David Winter, Lilliput Lane and Memories of Yesterday.

- **Business History:** Several years ago, Raymond W. and Ruthann Graham began collecting German nutcrackers. They experienced great difficulty in locating a good selection, which ultimately led to the formation of their store. Today, Graham's Crackers carries 400 different nutcrackers and smokers, ranging from $21-$4900! Collectors will enjoy the large selection of collectibles and the festive atmosphere at this store. Graham's Crackers specializes in unique and seasonal merchandise for <u>every</u> holiday, including its four showcases filled with hundreds of Russian nesting dolls. The shop is also a Redemption Center for numerous collector clubs. Graham's Crackers hosts many artist appearances and special events throughout the year. Raymond and Ruthann publish an attractive four-color publication, which is mailed to 19,000 collectors five times per year. Interested collectors can call to be placed on this mailing list.

• • • • • • •

The Great American Country Gift Store

29 Lafayette Road
Seacoast Village Mall
North Hampton, NH 03862
Phone: 603/964-9330

- **Store Hours:** Monday–Saturday: 10:00-5:00. Sunday: 12:00-5:00.

- **Secondary Market Lines:** Cat's Meow, Sarah's Attic, Lilliput Lane, Ladie & Friends, June McKenna, Possible Dreams, Attic Babies, Hudson Village, Department 56 Snowbabies.

- **Secondary Market Terms:** No consignments. Layaway. Mail orders. Drop shipments available. Free gift-wrapping.

- **Business History:** The Great American Country Gift Store specializes in collectibles and a whole lot more! In addition to carrying the lines listed above, this warm, inviting shop offers gourmet food items, candles, pottery and other gift items.

  Founded in 1988, this store specializes in the Cat's Meow secondary market. They are a Collector Club Redemption Center and offer special incentives to their Cat's Meow customers.

  The Great American Country Gift Store publishes a bi-annual newsletter which includes information on new collectibles from many manufacturers, as well as gift suggestions for upcoming holidays.

Great Gifts! Inc.

204 NE 1st Ave.
Hallandale, FL 33009
Phone: 305/454-9911

Great Gifts! Inc.
(That's Our Name)

- **Store Hours:** Monday–Saturday: 9:30-5:00.

- **Secondary Market Lines:** Swarovski, Lladro, Armani, Department 56: Dickens, Snow Village, Snowbabies; Precious Moments, Steiff.

- **Secondary Market Terms:** Consignment. 20% commission of sale. Listing service available.

- **Business History:** Family-owned and operated, Great Gifts! Inc. has been in business since 1983. They offer the collector a multitude of ways to sell their retired items, whether it be on consignment or by listing the collectible with this firm's match service. Great Gifts! carries a large inventory of Swarovski. If they don't have the retired item a collector is seeking, they will try to locate it. A member of Gift Creations Concepts, the firm is a Redemption Center for Swarovski, Lladro, Armani, Precious Moments, Enesco Musicals, Lilliput Lane and Ron Lee.

Great Lakes Gnome Exchange

7769 Silver Fox Drive
Boardman, OH 44512
Phone: 216/726-1400
Phone: 800/437-1476

- **Exchange Hours:** Monday–Friday: 4:00-10:00. Messages may be left 24 hours a day.

- **Secondary Market Lines:** Cairn Studios: Tom Clark, Tim Wolfe, Lee Sievers; John Hine Studios: Maurice Wideman.

- **Secondary Market Terms:** Members/sellers list collectibles for sale, plus 20% commission. Individual pieces, sets and entire collections are listed. Call for details.

Business History: Great Lakes specializes in Tom Clark Gnomes. Requests of member/subscribers caused the Exchange to expand by offering the works of Tim Wolfe, Lee Sievers and Maurice Wideman. The listings for Wideman not only include his *American Collection*, but also the Mark I variations of that collection, and his houses from the *Norwich Collection*.

The *Great Lakes Artwork Registry* is published ten times per membership year. The registry lists retired artwork, artwork of special interest (current and retired) and low- edition-number artwork. Informative articles highlight each issue, with the latest news about artists and their creations. Subscribers are encouraged to call the "Telegnome" listing update service at 216/726-6767. Each report includes new listings that are received between printings.

Greco Collectibles

3186-D So.Parker Road
Aurora, CO 80014
Phone: 303/755-6048

- **Store Hours:** Monday–Friday: 10:00-7:00. Saturday: 10:00-6:00. Sunday: 12:00-4:00.

- **Secondary Market Lines:** David Winter, Lilliput Lane, Sarah's Attic, Enesco Treasury Ornaments, Precious Moments, Chilmark Pewter. The firm's newsletter features a Collectors Exchange, where nearly all collectible lines may be listed.

- **Secondary Market Terms:** Broker's fee. Listings are free for three items. Call for details.

- **Business History:** Bernice and Harold Kessler entered the business world by starting a large gift and home furnishings store in 1972. They eventually moved to a smaller store, entering the collectibles market by selling through mail order in 1987. Today, Greco's is a well-established collectibles shop. They are a Redemption Center for Lilliput Lane, Precious Moments, Sarah's Attic, Jan Hagara, Enesco Musical Showcase and Land of Legends collectors clubs. They host six to eight artist shows and open houses each year.

The Kesslers publish 5,000 copies of their delightful and informative newsletter three times annually called "What's Mews." Collectors can read about recent product introductions and club activities, and have the opportunity to participate in Greco's popular Collectors Exchange.

The Handmaiden

P.O. Box 392
Fiskdale, MA 01518
Phone: 508/347-7757

- **Store Hours:** Daily: 10:00-6:00.

- **Secondary Market Lines:** June McKenna

- **Secondary Market Terms:** Buy outright. Some commission. Layaway available.

- **Business History:** Owner Brenda Higgins began collecting in 1985, four years after she opened The Handmaiden in 1981! The store carries several lines of collectibles and is a Redemption Center for Sarah's Attic, All God's Children and Cat's Meow.

  Brenda is an authority on the artwork of June McKenna and owns an extensive collection of the artist's dolls. In fact, the store features a lovely display of June McKenna's primary and retired artwork. June makes an artist appearance at The Handmaiden every November, having appeared the past five years. Additional open houses are held two to three times annually.

  The Handmaiden publishes a newsletter annually. Collectors may request a sample copy.

Heirlooms of Tomorrow

106 West Wilshire Avenue
Fullerton, CA 92632
Phone: 714/525-1522

- **Store Hours:** Tuesday–Saturday: 10:00-6:00.

- **Secondary Market Lines:** Gartlan USA, Marty Bell, Legends, Memories of Yesterday, David Winter.

- **Secondary Market Terms:** Consignments. Buy outright.

- **Business History:** Many collectors enjoy their hobby to such an extent that they turn that hobby into a business. That is just the case with Shereen Zerrenner and her recently formed store, Heirlooms of Tomorrow. Established in 1991, this store is a Redemption Center for Gartlan USA, David Winter, Memories of Yesterday and Marty Bell. Heirlooms of Tomorrow is a preferred dealer for Legends and a Heritage dealer for Memories of Yesterday. Artist appearances are held throughout the year.

  Shereen has bought and sold retired collectibles since 1982. She has taken this expertise and now runs a very active secondary market for the lines listed above. Interested collectors should call for more information.

• • • • • • •

Heirlooms of Tomorrow, Inc.

2178-1/2 NE 123rd St.
North Miami, FL 33181
Phone: 305/8990920
Orders: 800/544-2-BUY

Heirlooms of Tomorrow, Inc.
Specializing in Limited Edition Collectibles

- **Store Hours:** Monday: 12:00-5:30. Tuesday-Friday: 9:30-5:30. Saturday: 9:00-5:00.

- **Secondary Market Lines:** David Winter, ANRI, Hibel, Lladro, Goebel Miniatures, M.I. Hummel, Armani, Swarovski, Department 56, Cabbage Patch, Legends, Bradford, Krystonia, Precious Moments, Memories of Yesterday.

- **Secondary Market Terms:** Buy outright. Commission. Collectors should send a neatly written/typed list divided into buy/sell.

- **Business History:** With over ten years of experience and literally thousands of items, Heirlooms of Tomorrow is considered one of South Florida's foremost one-stop collectibles shops. The store is a family business, owned and operated by Pearl Finkelstein, an avid collector herself, with the help of her son, Norman as manager. Their helpful staff is always ready to help the collector in any way possible, making collecting a pleasure for their customers. Heirlooms of Tomorrow's long standing in the collectible field enables them to acquire many signed pieces, artist proofs, remarques and one-of-a-kinds by such famous artists as Edna Hibel, Robert Olszewski, M.I. Hummel and Sandra Kuck. With a booming mail order business, care is taken to ensure that collectibles will arrive safely, as they are shipped worldwide.

• • • • • • •

Hi Hat Collectibles

At East Town Antique Mall
6503 Slater Road
Chattanooga, TN 37412
Phone: 615/899-5498
Fax: 615/875-8945

- **Store Hours:** Monday–Saturday: 10:00-6:00. Sunday: 12:00-6:00.

- **Secondary Market Lines:** Goebel, Department 56, David Winter, Lilliput Lane, Lowell Davis, M.I. Hummel, Lladro, Royal Doulton, Raikes, Annalee, Steiff, All God's Children, John Sandridge, Tom Clark Gnomes, Jan Hagara, Maud Humphrey, Sebastian Miniatures, Hallmark, Coca Cola (various), Budweiser steins, Breyer horses, Chilmark, Cybis.

- **Secondary Market Terms:** Buy outright. Call for details.

- **Business History:** Carol and John Hudson have been in the antiques and collectibles business since 1979. Hi Hat Collectibles is located in their 18,000 square foot antique mall and provides full-service to collectors looking for both current and retired items.

  The Hudsons purchase collections and estates and conduct estate sales within a 150-mile radius of Chattanooga. They also provide appraisal services for both antiques and collectibles.

  Hi Hat invites inquiries on all lines of collectibles -- old and new -- and maintains an active "want" list for collectors.

• • • • • • •

House of Cards Limited

15425 Hall Road
Mt. Clemens, MI 48044
Phone: 313/247-2000

House of Cards Limited
Greeting Cards, Gifts & Collectibles

- **Store Hours:** Monday and Friday: 10:00-8:00. Tuesday-Thursday and Saturday: 10:00-5:00.

- **Secondary Market Lines:** Swarovski, Precious Moments, Memories of Yesterday, Lladro, M.I. Hummel, David Winter, Lilliput Lane, Maud Humphrey, Department 56: Snow Village, Heritage Village; plates.

- **Secondary Market Terms:** Consignments and out-right buys. Call for details.

- **Business History:** One of the largest Precious Moments secondary market dealers, House of Cards Limited is "home" for a large variety of collectibles. Owners Jim and Sue Haffey acknowledge that collectors began looking for retired artwork, and seeking these pieces has become this firm's specialty. In business since 1984, House of Cards is a Redemption Center for all clubs. The firm hosts a local chapter for Precious Moments called "Friends Forever" club. House of Cards is also a Distinguished Service Retailer for Enesco and holds open houses, featuring this manufacturer's products.

• • • • • • •

Hunt's Collectibles

595 Jackson Avenue
Satellite Beach, FL 32937
Phone: 407/777-1313
Fax: 407/777-1362

"The Hunt With Hounds"

- **Store Hours:** Monday–Saturday: 9:00-6:00.

- **Secondary Market Lines:** Goebel Miniatures.

- **Secondary Market Terms:** Buy outright. Collectors seeking a hard-to-find Olszewski figurine, may likely locate it in stock at Hunt's, or their locator service will find it in a timely manner.

- **Business History:** Since 1983, Hunt's Collectibles has specialized exclusively in the Goebel Miniatures line by famed miniaturist Robert Olszewski. Dick Hunt is the author of the book *The Goebel Miniatures of Robert Olszewski*, an authoritative reference and price guide.

Imagine That!

5903 Queens Chapel Rd.
Hyattsville, MD 20782-3072
Phone: 800/223-5903
Phone: 301/699-0928

- **Store Hours:** Answering Machine: 24-hours, Human Contact: After 5:00pm and usually all day weekends and holidays.

- **Secondary Market Lines:** Land of Legend, Enchantica, Pocket Dragons, Perth Pewter, Gallo, Rawcliffe, Hap Henriksen's Wizards & Dragons, Hudson, Chilmark, All Major Art Print Publishers, Western, Wildlife, Nature's Heritage, Erte, Lilliput Lane, David Winter.

- **Secondary Market Terms:** Specializes in the location of hard-to-find retired collectibles and prints. Art print and collectible search service is free! Seller/buyer contacts usually provided free of charge, if available.

- **Business History:** Imagine That! offers 100% satisfaction guaranteed. They specialize in fantasy, wildlife and western art. This business also handles a variety of contemporary art, i.e. Erte, Leroy Neiman, etc. They also import Border Fine Arts.

  Imagine That! generally offers all of the services a gallery and/or collectibles store would offer...but through the convenience of the mail. They offer a full range of services, including conservation framing and free appraisals for insurance purposes, if items are purchased from this establishment. They honor most Collector Club Redemption Certificates, especially Lilliput Lane, David Winter, Land of Legend and Enchantica.

International House

15802 La Grange Road
Orland Park, IL 60462
Phone: 708/349-3366

2827 West Aurora Avenue
Naperville, IL 60540
Phone: 708/717-5002

- **Store Hours:** Monday–Friday: 10:00-9:00. Saturday: 10:00-6:00. Sunday: 11:00-5:00.

- **Secondary Market Lines:** Annalee, Department 56, Duncan Royale, Precious Moments, Memories of Yesterday, Emmett Kelly Jr., David Winter, Legends, Lilliput Lane, Lladro, Swarovski, M.I. Hummel, plates, dolls.

- **Secondary Market Terms:** No consignments. Buy outright. Specializes in locating hard-to-find collectibles.

- **Business History:** In business since 1976, International House is a collectible and gift retailer, carrying over 200 different collectible lines! Service is very important to this firm, and it shows. The staff at both stores are courteous, friendly and knowledgeable about both the primary and secondary markets.

  Several open houses and special events are planned annually. Over the years, the stores have received visits from every major artist in the business, including Enesco sculptors, ANRI woodcarvers and Swarovski sculptors. International House is a Showcase Department 56 dealer, and a leader in the collectibles industry.

  Customers receive mailings on retirements, new product releases and shows, in addition to receiving catalogs and newsletters.

• • • • • • •

Intrigue Gift Shop

P.O. Box 2147 112 E. Elkhorn Avenue
Estes Park, CO 80517
Phone: Consumer questions: 303/586-4217
Phone: Orders only: 800/735-GIFT

- **Store Hours:** Open every day!

- **Secondary Market Lines:** Chilmark, Legends, Don
  Polland, Tom Clark Gnomes, Lladro, All God's Children,
  Sarah's Attic, Armani, Lowell Davis, The Disney Collection,
  Mark Hopkins' Bronzes, Maud Humphrey, Emmett Kelly, Jr.,
  Ron Lee Clowns, Thomas Kinkade prints, Maruri, Melody in
  Motion, Wee Forest Folk, David Winter, Lilliput Lane.

- **Secondary Market Terms:** Locater service.

- **Business History:** Nestled in the heart of the majestic
  Colorado Rockies, just minutes from the Rocky Mountain
  National Park, lies the quaint village of Estes Park, Colorado.
  There awaits a collector's dream: Intrigue Gift Shop.
  Established in 1969, they have developed an internationally
  renowned reputation as a leader concerning the diversity
  and the completeness of their collector lines. These lines
  have been carefully selected, not only for their immediate
  aesthetic value, but also for their enduring investment
  potential. Intrigue's knowledgeable staff takes great pleasure in ensuring that the experience had by both the avid
  collector and the novice is a memorable one. The shop hosts
  numerous artist appearances throughout the year. The
  Intrigue Gift Shop is a Redemption Center for many of the
  lines listed above, in addition to offering free gift-wrapping
  and direct shipping for those special occasions.

• • • • • • •

Island Treasures

2845 Richmond Avenue
Staten Island, NY 10314
Phone: 718/698-1234
Fax: 718/698-1888

Island Treasures
The Collectors' Showplace

- **Store Hours:** Monday–Sat.: 10:00-6:00. Sunday: 12:00-4:00.

- **Secondary Market Lines:** Plates, dolls, Department 56, Precious Moments, Perillo, Memories of Yesterday, Swarovski, M.I. Hummel, Goebel Miniatures, Emmett Kelly, Jr., David Winter, Lilliput Lane, Lowell Davis.

- **Secondary Market Terms:** Buy outright. Commission. Trade.

- **Business History:** Island Treasures, a full-service collectibles store, first opened in 1978. The owners loved collecting and wanted to share the idea that collectibles make beautiful home decor items and have the potential of a good investment. Island Treasures has approximately six to eight open houses annually. They have featured Gregory Perillo, Sandra Kuck, Yolanda Bello, Emmett Kelly, Jr. and Hummel artists, to name a few. Their open houses include Precious Moments, Memories of Yesterday, Swarovski, Lladro, Department 56, Bradford plates, etc. They are a Redemption Center and authorized dealer for the lines above in addition to Perillo, Maud Humphrey, Krystonia, Sports Impressions, Jan Hagara, All God's Children, Ron Lee, EKJ, Lowell Davis, Annalee, Lilliput Lane, Armani, Enesco Music boxes and more. They are also a Showcase store for Department 56, a Distinguished Service Retailer for Enesco, a Heritage Center for Memories of Yesterday, Maud Humphrey Gallery store and a top Bradford Dealer.

• • • • • •

Jerdón

311 S. Main
Carthage, MO 64836
Phone: 417/358-3343

JERDÓN

- **Store Hours:** Retail shop always open Thursday-Saturday 10:00-5:00. Other days by appointment or by chance. Office open Tuesday-Saturday.

- **Secondary Market Lines:** Precious Moments, Lowell Davis, Hallmark.

- **Secondary Market Terms:** Buy outright. Limited brokerage.

- **Business History:** Located halfway between the homes of Sam Butcher and Lowell Davis in Carthage, Jerdón is an entire block-long store, sitting across from one of the most beautiful court-houses in the country! Owners Don and Gerri Green handle private liquidation of estates and large collections. They work with indi-viduals nationwide and handle many of their secondary market transactions by phone. Collectors visiting this store, though, are in for a visual treat, as the merchandise changes daily. Customers are likely to see the artwork of Jan Hagara, Tom Clark, M.I. Hummel, Lladro, Royal Copenhagen, Royal Doulton, Bossons, Memories of Yesterday and Christmas ornaments. The Greens always maintain a large inventory of retired Precious Moments, Lowell Davis and Hallmark. They specialize in first marks, retired and suspended pieces. The staff are members of the American Society of Appraisers, and utilize the Collectors' Information Bureau's Price Guide, whose values help the firm extablish a fair and accurate price for buyers and sellers.

Jiana Inc.

Union Market
2445 Springfield Ave.
Union, NJ 07083
Phone: 908/964-4600 (store)
Phone: 201/492-1728 (office)
Fax: 201/492-8069

- **Store Hours:** Friday & Saturday: 11:00-9:00. Sunday: 11:00-6:00.

- **Secondary Market Lines:** Armani, Annalee, Alex Haley, Sarah's Attic, Department 56, Swarovski, Ron Lee, Lilliput Lane, Maruri, Silver Deer, Enesco, Bradford Exchange.

- **Secondary Market Terms:** Buy outright or consignment.

- **Business History:** Jiana, Inc. has grown considerably over the past few years and has become a full-service collectibles showcase gallery. They are authorized dealers for most of the top collectibles lines, and collectors may join or renew club memberships and redeem club member pieces through Jiana.

Jiana specializes in the artwork of the famous Italian artist, Giuseppe Armani, and is one of the largest authorized dealers in New Jersey. They have about 250 Armani figurines on display at all times, including many retired pieces. Store owner, Diana Madarasz, has been an avid collector of Armani's work for over fifteen years and possesses a great deal of knowledge regarding these figurines. Last year, the store participated in an event where Mr. Armani personally met customers and signed their figurines.

• • • • • • •

Juliet's Collectibles

128 N. Glassell
Orange, CA 92666
Phone: 714/633-4438

Juliet's Collectibles

- **Store Hours:** Tuesday-Sunday: 10:30-5:30.

- **Secondary Market Lines:** Ashton-Drake dolls, All God's Children, David Winter, M.I. Hummel, Sarah's Attic, Tom Clark, Wee Forest Folk, graphics: Terry Redlin, Zolan, Sandra Kuck, Corinne Layton.

- **Secondary Market Terms:** Buy outright. Consignment. 90-day layaway. Free shipping in continental U.S.

- **Business History:** Juliet's Collectibles was opened in 1967 by Juliet Boysen. The store has one of the largest selections of All God's Children in the southern California area and is a Redemption Center for Sarah's Attic, Tom Clark Gnomes, M.I. Hummel, ANRI, David Winter and All God's Children. Juliet's also carries a complete line of frames, stands, and hangers. The knowledgeable staff will assist in arranging collectors' artwork.

  Juliet's publishes a quarterly newsletter which collectors can receive, just by calling the store. Open houses are also hosted four times annually.

  Customer service is important to Juliet Boysen, and she makes every effort to assist collectors in locating retired items. In fact, she will continue listing items until she locates them or until the collector wishes to discontinue the search. Juliet's has many retired Bradford plates and back issues of M.I. Hummel .

Just Browsing/ Village Christmas Shoppe

28200 U.S. Highway 189, Suite F-100
P.O. Box 1686
Lake Arrowhead, CA 92352
Phone: 714/337-8322
Phone: 909/337-8322 (after Nov., 1992)

- **Store Hours:** Daily: 10:00-5:30.

- **Secondary Market Lines:** Legends, Duncan Royale, Precious Moments, Memories of Yesterday, Enesco Treasury of Christmas Ornaments, Fontanini by Roman.

- **Secondary Market Terms:** Call the store for details.

- **Business History:** Located in the snow-capped San Bernadino mountains just off the Rim of the World Highway, Just Browsing has called Lake Arrowhead "home" since 1981. Collectors will enjoy 'browsing' through the shop, in addition to attending open houses throughout the year.

  This store has been active in the Duncan Royale secondary market for five years. In fact, they are one of the few stores in the country to display a full set of *History of Santa Claus I* figurines. Just Browsing has also been active in Legends' secondary market for the past three years.

  The owners of Just Browsing made a dream a reality when they opened The Christmas Shoppe in May 1991. This festive shop carries a wide variety of holiday collectibles from such manufacturers as Midwest Importers, House of Hatten, Enesco and Roman, featuring Fontanini nativities.

● ● ● ● ● ● ●

Justin Porterfield, LTD.

17350 East Seventeenth Street
Tustin, CA 92680
Phone: 714/544-5223
Phone: 714/544-7649

Justin porterfield, ltd.

- **Store Hours:** Monday–Friday:10:00-6:00. Saturday: 10:00-5:30. Sunday: 11:00-4:00.

- **Secondary Market Lines:** Madame Alexander dolls, Thomas Kinkade, Marty Bell.

- **Secondary Market Terms:** Purchases and consignments.

- **Business History:** Judy Anderson has touched the hearts of many collectors by providing a nostalgic store, where her customers can shop for high-end home decor, gifts and collectibles, in addition to spending a delightful afternoon in her loft-turned-tearoom for an elegantly served high English tea.

Gift ideas abound at Justin Porterfield, as the store is filled with cases, shelves and curios displaying beautiful merchandise, and the loft is no exception. Flowers grace the cozy tables, and graphics provide added beauty to the atmosphere, as tea is catered three times per week by "Persnickatea."

Judy's interest and knowledge spill over into the secondary market, as she assists collectors nationwide in their quest to locate retired artwork.

Kabet's

1901 N.W. Expressway #1030 Penn Sq.
Oklahoma City, OK 73118
Phone: 405/842-2242
Phone: 800/4-KABETS

- **Store Hours:** Monday–Saturday: 10:00-9:00, Sunday: 1:00-6:00.

- **Secondary Market Lines:** Duncan Royale, Precious Moments, Vienna bronzes, Russian lacquer.

- **Secondary Market Terms:** Buy outright. Layaway is available.

- **Business History:** Kabet's has been in operation for 35 years. They are the oldest, in fact, the first gift shop in Oklahoma! This 4,500 square foot facility houses a full line of collectibles as well as beautiful antiques on display. They are a redemption center for the lines listed above and host about six artist/open houses annually. Locating lines the collector has never set eyes upon is a challenge readily accepted by owner Prudy Gorrell and her staff.

• • • • • • •

Karolson's Treasures

312 E. Market Street
Leesburg, VA 22075
Phone: 703/771-1776

Karolson's Treasures

- **Store Hours:** Tuesday–Saturday: 10:00-6:00. Sunday: 12:00-5:00. Closed Mondays.

- **Secondary Market Lines:** David Winter, Lilliput Lane, Tom Clark, Krystonia, Duncan Royale, Cat's Meow.

- **Secondary Market Terms:** No consignments. Buy outright. Shipping available.

- **Business History:** Karolson's Treasures opened for business in 1985. The shop is located in Leesburg, Virginia. The town is a quaint, historical and friendly community 35 miles east of Washington D.C. The store initially operated as an antique and collectible enterprise. In 1988, the antique section of the store was phased out. This transition was necessary due to the rapidly growing collectible lines. In 1991, Karolson's Treasures received the "Distinguished Achievement Award" for innovative display of David Winter Cottages from the John Hine Studios in Houston. The display is one of the most extensive of primary and secondary market cottages in Northern Virginia.

  Many secondary market creations by Tom Clark are also prominently displayed and available to the collector. Karol Olson is on the premises during business hours to offer to collectors information and history of the artists, covering the wide range of collectibles available at the shop.

• • • • • • •

Keepsakes & Kollectibles

219-A Gentry
Spring, TX 77373
Phone: 713/353-9233

- **Store Hours:** Monday–Saturday: 10:00-5:00. Sunday: 12:00-5:00.

- **Secondary Market Lines:** All God's Children, Sarah's Attic, Swarovski, Lladro, Armani, Precious Moments, Memories of Yesterday, Jan Hagara.

- **Secondary Market Terms:** Consignments. Buy outright. Locator service. Call for details.

- **Business History:** While living and working overseas, Steve and Peggy Wall collected Asian antiques. In 1982, they bought The Brass Corner and eventually changed the name to Keepsakes & Kollectibles, adding collectibles to the store's long list of high quality items. Located in Historic Old Town in Spring, are over 125 shops in a village atmosphere, with some buildings dating back to the 1800s. Keepsakes is located in an old renovated schoolhouse, which is decorated at Christmas time in an old fashioned holiday motif. The store is a Redemption Center for the lines listed above, in addition to Maud Humphrey, Sports Impressions, Alex Haley, Krystonia, Enchantica, Fontanini, Sandicast, Frumps, and Enesco musicals. A member of NALED, Keepsakes hosts artist appearances several times per year, inviting artists such as Sarah Schultz, Maurice Wideman and Martha Holcombe. Newsletters are published quarterly, featuring new product releases, club news, market news and more.

The Kent Collection

3401 South Lincoln Street
Englewood, CO 80110
Phone: 303/761-0059

- **Store Hours:** Tuesday–Saturday: 10:00-5:00. Seven days a week in December.

- **Secondary Market Lines:** De Grazia, Rockwell, Terry Redlin, Maud Humphrey, Ozz Franca, Memories of Yesterday, Sarah's Attic, Fred Stone, Gregory Perillo.

- **Secondary Market Terms:** No consignments. Each "seek or search" is a challenge and each request receives special consideration. Deposits required before search is begun -- refunded in full if item is not found.

- **Business History:** The Kent Collection was established in 1977 in Denver, Colorado by Reda Walsh and continues today as a retail store selling limited edition collectibles, greeting cards and gifts. No antiques are sold at the shop. The Kent Collection is a member of the National Association of Limited Edition Dealers(NALED), and Reda has served on the Board of Directors for this organization. The Kent Collection was one of the very first dealer members to be appointed by The Bradford Exchange when a dealer network was initiated. The store is a Redemption Center for several collector clubs, including M.I. Hummel, Memories of Yesterday, Maud Humphrey and the Lowell Davis Farm Club.

• • • • • • •

La Maison Capri, Inc.

1715 Boardwalk
Atlantic City, NJ 08401
Phone: 609/345-4305

LA MAISON CAPRI
14K GOLD · OBJECTS OF ART · JEWELRY · AUDIO · GIFTS

- **Store Hours:** Open 7 days a week. 10:00-5:00-Winter, 10:00-8:00-Summer.

- **Secondary Market Lines:** Ron Lee, Department 56, Emmett Kelly, Jr., M.I. Hummel, Lladro, Armani, Swarovski, Miss Martha Originals, Precious Moments.

- **Secondary Market Terms:** Buy outright. Call for details.

- **Business History:** Located in a resort area, La Maison Capri, Inc. has become a national source for collectibles.

  Established in 1976, La Maison Capri, Inc. grew from a small porcelain gift shop to the present premiere collectible gallery. Their highly trained staff has created a personable atmosphere, and great customer relationships have evolved.

  Mr. Joe Hayoun, in-house appraiser, provides locals as well as out-of-state collectors with expert appraisals and advice on their collections.

• • • • • • •

Bob Lamson
Beer Steins, Inc.

509 N. 22nd Street
Allentown, PA 18104
Phone: 215/435-8611
Phone: 800/435-8611

**BOB LAMSON
BEER STEINS, Inc.**

- **Store Hours:** Monday–Friday: 9:00-9:00. Saturday: 10:00-4:00. Other hours by appointment.

- **Secondary Market Lines:** Anheuser-Busch: Michelob, Budweiser, Bud Light, etc.; Coors, Strohs, Miller, Heineken, Hamm's, Pabst, Olympia steins and related collectibles with other beer affiliations.

- **Secondary Market Terms:** Buy/Sell/Trade. Terms available upon request for larger purchases. Please inquire.

- **Business History:** Bob Lamson Beer Steins, Inc. was incorporated in 1990. Prior to that time, the Lamson family had been collectors of Breweriana and beer steins for over twenty years. The corporation is owned and operated solely by the Lamson family: Shirley A. Lamson, president; Lisa Lamson Pecsek, vice-president; and Jodi Lamson Scanlan, secretary-treasurer. The company has a retail store located in Allentown, Pennsylvania and also ships orders to every state in the nation and to Canada. Most orders are processed and shipped the same week. Price lists are mailed to customers throughout the year or on a request basis. If an item is not on a price list, collectors are invited to contact the company, who will try to locate the piece for the best possible price. Collectors should call with any additional questions they have regarding the company or stein collecting.

• • • • • • •

Lancelot's

1700 E. Douglas
Wichita, KS 67214
Phone: 316/267-3206
Fax: 316/267-3738

Lancelot's

- **Store Hours:** January-October, Monday–Saturday: 9:30-5:30.
November-December: Sunday 1:00-5:00.

- **Secondary Market Lines:** M.I. Hummel, Lladro,
Duncan Royale, Flambro, Emmett Kelly Jr., Lilliput Lane, David
Winter, Department 56, All God's Children, Precious Moments,
Tom Clark Gnomes, Armani.

- **Secondary Market Terms:** No consignments. Buy
outright. Call manager, Yvonne Bensch for details.

- **Business History:** The Lancelot Tile Co., founded in
1950, grew into a specialty store with an unbelievable product mix including collectibles, ceramic tile, fireplace and bar-
becue equipment and patio furniture. Mrs. Lancelot entered
the collectibles market in 1970 because of her love for ceram-
ics. Today, Lancelot's primary market includes Lladro, M.I.
Hummel, All God's Children, Miss Martha's Originals, Alex
Haley, Laura's Attic, Sarah's Attic, Armani, glass and Goebel
eggs and angels, Precious Moments, Duncan Royale, Cairn
Gnomes, DeGrazia and Emmett Kelly, Sr., Emmett Kelly Jr.
and Roman. They also carry David Winter, Lilliput Lane,
Maurice Wideman, and they are a Showcase Dealer for
Department 56. Lancelot's also sells plates and bells from
Schmid, Hummel, Bing & Grondahl and Royal Copenhagen.
The store is a Redemption Center for many of the lines listed
above. Yvonne Bensch, collectibles manager, and Ernestine
Lancelot, owner, are appraisers, and Lancelot's also offers a
restoration service.

The Ron Lee Gallery

Radisson Hotel
999 Enchanted Way
Simi Valley, CA 93065
Phone: 805/520-8488
Phone: 800/829-3934

- **Store Hours:** Monday-Thursday: 7:30-2:30, 5:00-9:00. Friday: 7:30-2:30, 6:00-10:00. Saturday: 8:00-2:30, 6:00-10:00. Sunday: 8:00-2:30.

- **Secondary Market Lines:** RON LEE clown, circus theme and cartoon character sculptures, figurines and limited editions.

- **Secondary Market Terms:** No consignments. Buy outright. Call for details.

- **Business History:** Owned and operated by the sculptor/manufacturer and his wife, Jill, the Ron Lee Gallery was originally opened to provide a showcase for sculptures created at the Ron Lee's World of Clowns factory located in Simi Valley. Encouraged by a warm welcome from the community at large and collectors, the intimate Gallery presents one of the largest collections and selections of figurine art ever displayed by one artist. Patrons of the gallery are welcome to tour the factory to see how Ron Lee creations come to life. Delivering personalized service, sales personnel are very dedicated and knowledgeable about Ron Lee art. Lucky patrons may also meet Ron Lee as they browse the Gallery on any given day. All secondary market transactions are conducted by the staff, under the direct supervision of the Gallery manager, and independent of the gallery owners.

The Lemon Tree

636 Parkway
Gatlinburg, TN 37738
Phone: 615/436-4602
Fax: 615/436-5783

Since 1972

- **Store Hours:** Monday–Saturday: 9:00am-11:00 pm.

- **Secondary Market Lines:** Department 56: All villages and Snowbabies, Emmett Kelly, Jr., Duncan Royale, David Winter, M.I. Hummel, Lowell Davis, Precious Moments, Lilliput Lane, Lladro, Cabbage Patch.

- **Secondary Market Terms:** Commission added to collectors' sales price.

- **Business History:** Over the span of twenty years, The Lemon Tree has grown from a small gift shop in the heart of the Great Smoky Mountains, to one of the nation's leading showcases, providing personal service and top line collectibles.

  Publisher of three annual newsletters, The Lemon Tree has expanded to collectors nationwide through their mail order division. They have an extensive list of lines, including those mentioned above and more.

  The Lemon Tree Collectors' Club offers numerous benefits, including exclusive specials on Department 56 merchandise and two reunions annually, one the first Saturday each May and one at The Gatlinburg Christmas Faire during Thanksgiving week.

• • • • • • •

Lena's Gift Gallery

137 E. 4th Avenue
San Mateo, CA 94401
Phone: 415/342-8848
Phone: 800/231-9517

- **Store Hours:** Tuesday–Friday: 9:30-5:30. Sat.: 10:00-5:00.

- **Secondary Market Lines:** Bradford plates, ANRI, Tom Clark Gnomes, P. Buckley Moss, Penni Anne Cross, M.I. Hummel, Wee Forest Folk.

- **Secondary Market Terms:** Locator service, specializing in plates and figurines.

- **Business History:** In 1971, Judy Lena's interest in collectibles was piqued, when she bought her granddaughter the first issue in the M.I. Hummel annual plate series. By 1974, Judy opened a mail order plate business and did so well that she eventually shared a storefront with an antique dealer. As the business grew, Judy continued to move and expand the business.

  Today, Lena's Gift Gallery is a full-service collectibles store. Judy maintains that her collector's mentality helps her to better understand her customers. Her goal is to help them enjoy their hobby. She offers decorating tips, hosts open houses and mails postcards, catalogs and newsletters to interested collectors. Lena's Gift Gallery also features a custom framing department for graphics and plates. Collectors are invited to call for brochures and to place orders by mail. Living in earthquake country, Judy is an expert in locating back issues to replace broken items or can assist collectors in locating collectibles to fill in their series.

The Limited Edition

2170 Sunrise Highway
Merrick, NY 11566
Phone: 516/623-4400
Phone: 800/645-2864
Fax: 516/867-3701

- **Store Hours:** Monday–Saturday: 10:00-6:00. Friday: 10:00-9:00.

- **Secondary Market Lines:** Precious Moments, Department 56: Heritage Villages and Snowbabies; Lladro, M.I. Hummel, Lowell Davis, Swarovski.

- **Secondary Market Terms:** No consignments. Buy outright. Collectors should call with asking price.

- **Business History:** Over the past 18 years, The Limited Edition has become one of the most important sources of primary and secondary market collectibles in the country. Many collectible companies recommend The Limited Edition to collectors as a source for locating their artwork. This includes collectors throughout the United States, as well as countries such as Singapore, Norway, Germany and Australia.

The Limited Edition has developed a very knowledgeable and caring sales staff, in addition to which, three separate departments have been created within the store. These departments are : Precious Moments, The World of Department 56 and Collectors Plates. When collectors call regarding any of these collectibles, their call is transferred to the specific department in order to assist in the most efficient manner. All purchases are recorded on computer so that collectors can be informed of new releases, retired items, limited editions, special offers and more.

Lita Sale Import

15565 Eilers Rd.
Aurora, OR 97002
Phone: 503/678-1622

- **Hours:** Monday–Friday: 9:00-6:00. Call anytime (preferably during waking hours). Showroom open by appointment only.

- **Secondary Market Lines:** Annette Himstedt dolls, Ulbricht and Steinbach nutcrackers, Uta Brauser Porcelain dolls.

- **Secondary Market Terms:** Buy and sell outright.

- **Business History:** As a result of her daughters' involvement in dancing with *The Nutcracker Ballet* and her love of collecting nutcrackers and dolls, Lita Sale decided to start an import company, which is located 20 miles south of Portland. When German doll artist, Annette Himstedt, began exporting her doll line in 1987, Lita immediately became involved with these dolls in this country, as she was very knowledgeable about the artist, the dollmaking process and the dolls' phenomenal collectibility.

  Each year, Lita attends the International Toy Fair in Nuremberg, Germany, where she meets many of the artists in their homes, studios, and factories. Lita has also watched some of the artists create their collectibles, a privilege indeed, as processes and ideas are tightly guarded and rarely shared with the public.

  The firm publishes a newsletter, including information on new and retired products and a price list.

• • • • • • •

Lori's Collectibles

6121 E. Broadway #134
Tucson, AZ 85711
Phone: 602/790-6668 (information)
Phone: 800/458-6668 Extension 12 (orders)

Lori's
COLLECTIBLES
"A store where the vast selection is an adventure"

- **Store Hours:** Tuesday-Friday: 10:00-6:00. Saturday: 10:00-5:00. Closed Sunday and Monday.

- **Secondary Market Lines:** Bradford Plates, Lladro, M.I. Hummel, Lowell Davis, ANRI, Department 56, including Snowbabies, Royal Doulton, Precious Moments, David Winter, Olaf Wieghorst lithos, Zolan lithos, Lilliput Lane, Chilmark, Legends, Bossons, Wideman, DeGrazia, Krystonia, Memories of Yesterday, Ashton-Drake, Gartlan USA, Rockwell, Gorham, Goebel Miniatures, Tom Clark, Fontanini, Swarovski, Sarah's Attic.

- **Secondary Market Terms:** Buy outright on selected merchandise. Locator service. Will work with other dealers. Call for details.

- **Business History:** Lori Gerber began collecting when she was only fourteen years old, and that interest never waned. In 1982, she converted her hobby into a full-fledged business, which continues to grow by leaps and bounds. Lori's husband, Hy, who is a businessman by trade, eventually joined Lori, as the store expanded. Lori's carries a full line of collectibles, adding about two new lines per year. The store is a Redemption Center for many of the lines listed above and hosts several open houses during the year. A newsletter is published frequently, and interested collectors can be placed on the mailing list. Lori's offers personalized service, integrity and fair secondary market prices.

Mader's

Mader's Tower Gallery
1041 N. Old World Third Street
Milwaukee, WI 53203
Phone: 414/271-1911

- **Store Hours:** Daily: 11:00-9:00.

- **Secondary Market Lines:** M.I. Hummel figurines.

Mader's Old World Third Street Gallery
1025 N. Old World Third St.
Milwaukee, WI 53203
Phone: 414/278-0088
- **Store Hours:** Monday-Saturday: 11:00-7:00. Sunday: 11:00-5:00.

- **Secondary Market Lines:** Prints by Bateman, Brenders, Gromme.

- **Secondary Market Terms:** Consignment. Buy outright. Call for details.

- **Business History:** Celebrating their 90th year, Mader's galleries have added many new lines and artists in the past few years. They appraise M.I. Hummel and Berta Hummel figurines and plates and are a Redemption Center for Lladro and Hummel. The Old World Third Street Gallery features works by Bateman, Brenders, Gromme, Calle, Peterson and Clayton-Weirs. Both galleries host artist appearances and open houses.

• • • • • • •

Mar-Cher Plates

5486 Riverside Dr.
Chino, CA 91710
Phone: 714/628-3381

- **Store Hours:** Monday–Friday: 10:00-5:00. Saturday: 11:00-4:00.

- **Secondary Market Lines:** Limited Edition plates: Bradford, Hamilton, Reco; Ashton-Drake Dolls, Jan Hagara, Sports Impressions, Precious Moments, Lowell Davis, Enesco Ornaments, lithographs.

- **Secondary Market Terms:** Buy outright. Call for details.

- **Business History:** Mar-Cher Plates has grown significantly in the last ten years, from about 50 limited edition plates, to one of the largest selections of collectibles in the Inland Empire. Mar-Cher especially features a large line of Bradford Exchange plates and of Ashton-Drake dolls. Custom framing is available for collectors' favorite plates. Mar-Cher Plates has conducted open houses in the past with artists Yolando Bello, Cathy Hippensteel, Jan Hagara and Suzie Morton.

• • • • • • •

Martha's Exchange Service

Specialists in National Secondary Services

3451 Queens St. Suite 634
Sarasota, FL 34231
Phone: 813/925-8214

Martha's
Exchange Service

- **Store Hours:** Monday–Friday: 9:00-5:00.

- **Secondary Market Lines:** Department 56: Dickens Village, New England Village, Christmas in the City, Alpine Village, North Pole Village, Snow Village, Snowbabies; David Winter, Lilliput Lane, Maud Humphrey, Duncan Royale, Emmett Kelly, Jr., Lowell Davis, Tom Clark Gnomes, Swarovski, Original Disney Animation Art.

- **Secondary Market Terms:** 10% commission. Consignments are accepted for their monthly shows. Call for more details.

- **Business History:** Martha's Exchange Service is a family business. They are associated with four shops called "Martha's Candy and Clutter," located in Sarasota and Venice, Florida and one in Richmond, Virginia. They have been in business since 1982 and have run the exchange for four years.

  Martha's Exchange is one of the largest secondary markets for Department 56, David Winter, Lilliput Lane and Swarovski. They work with retailers and exchanges throughout the country, while assisting collectors in locating retired collectibles. The firm furnishes references upon request and welcomes calls from their clients.

• • • • • • •

Marty's Secondary Market Sales

1869 Marcus Ct.
Hayward, CA 94541
Phone: 510/881-1256
Phone: 800/742-7119

- **Store Hours:** Monday–Friday: 9:00-6:00. Saturday: 9:00-12:00.

- **Secondary Market Lines:** All God's Children, Sarah's Attic, Lowell Davis, Maud Humphrey, Jan Hagara figurines and dolls, M.I. Hummel, Precious Moments, Swarovski.

- **Secondary Market Terms:** No subscription or membership fees to join. No cost, no obligation listings. Nationwide contacts. Low brokerage rates: Over $500- 15%; under $500-20%.

- **Business History:** Marty's Secondary Market Sales is a secondary market listing service for collectors. It is a service designed to assist collectors in buying or selling limited edition or retired collectibles. Their service does not stock or keep inventory. It relies, instead, on collectors who wish to sell their items. Available to dealers and collectors, it is a service only. Only items that are limited, suspended or retired are listed through this service.

  Owner Maurcena ("Marty") M. Lee began collecting in 1989, and it was through her hobby that she discovered a need for her secondary market service. Research on some pieces takes three to six months. Collectors interested in receiving a complimentary price list should send a self-addressed stamped envelope.

Memories In Motion

114 Clark Avenue
Elkton, VA 22827
Phone: 703/298-9234, after 6:00p.m.

Memories In Motion M

- **Office Hours:** Mail order only: Call 6:00-9:00pm weekdays. 9:00-9:00 weekends and holidays.

- **Secondary Market Lines:** Hallmark Christmas and Easter ornaments, Hallmark Merry Miniatures, David Winter Christmas ornaments.

- **Secondary Market Terms:** Extensive networking system. Locates items not in stock. No consignments. Buys outright when needed. Convenient layaway plan. Publishes a price list. Call for details.

- **Business History:** Memories In Motion is a mail order business nestled at the foot of the Blue Ridge Mountains in the beautiful Shenandoah Valley of Virginia. Owner, Bobbie Ann Horne believes in doing business the old-fashioned way. She is easy to talk with and serves her clients with honesty and warmth. Says Bobbie Ann, "I'm small enough to add a personal touch, but large enough to meet the needs of collectors." Bobbie Ann started her mail order business in 1990 and now has clients all across the United States, in Canada, Mexico and around the world. She is a charter member of the Hallmark Keepsake Ornament Collector's Club, serves as a consultant to local Hallmark stores and is available as a speaker to groups and clubs.

• • • • • • •

Miller's Hallmark & Gift Gallery

1322 N. Barron St.
Eaton, OH 45320
Phone: 513/456-4151

$\boxed{\text{Miller's Gift Gallery}}$

- **Store Hours:** Monday–Friday: 9:00-9:00. Saturday: 9:00-6:00. Sunday: 12:00-5:00.

- **Secondary Market Lines:** Swarovski, Lladro, Memories of Yesterday, M.I. Hummel, Precious Moments, Goebel Miniatures, Hallmark Ornaments, Hallmark Galleries, Miss Martha's Originals, Sports Impressions, David Winter, Maurice Wideman, Caithness Paperweights, Maud Humphrey, Walt Disney Classics.

- **Secondary Market Terms:** No consignments. Buy outright. Call for details.

- **Business History:** Miller's Hallmark & Gift Gallery has grown significantly through the years, from a specialty store with only M.I. Hummel figurines, into a full service Hallmark and collectibles showcase gallery. This store provides collectors with expert appraisal services. Dean A. Genth is an Associate Member of the American Society of Appraisers-Dayton, Ohio Chapter. He has been actively appraising M. I. Hummel figurines for over 15 years. Private and personal appraisals are done by Mr. Genth for individuals needing current valuations of their collections for insurance purposes. The Miller Company and Dean A. Genth have served as counsel to many insurance companies and individuals that need expert advice on matters related to collectibles.

The Mole Hole of Kalamazoo

300 South Kalamazoo Mall
Kalamazoo, MI 49007
Phone: 616/344-9000
Fax: 616/344-6623

THE MOLE HOLE

- **Store Hours:** Monday–Friday: 10:00-6:00. Saturday: 10:00-5:00. Sunday: 12:00-5:00.

- **Secondary Market Lines:** Department 56: All Villages and accessories; Duncan Royale, Sarah's Attic, Iris Arc, David Winter, Chilmark, Krystonia.

- **Secondary Market Terms:** Buy outright. Commission. Call for details.

- **Business History:** The Mole Hole of Kalamazoo was established by Jere Hinman in 1984. This 4,000 square-foot facility offers a variety of gifts, from the light-hearted to the sophisticated, in addition to numerous collectible lines. Home decor items are also featured.

  The Mole Hole is a Diamond dealer for Duncan Royale and a Showcase dealer for Department 56. They are a Redemption Center for Krystonia, Sarah's Attic, David Winter, Duncan Royale, Iris Arc and Rick Cain.

  Open houses are held once annually in November to ring in the Christmas season. Sales representatives from various manufacturers visit with collectors and answer their questions during this festive affair.

• • • • • • •

The Morgan Co.

6301 Highbanks Rd.
Mascoutah, IL 62258
Phone: 618/566-7568 - information
Phone: 800/422-4510 - orders
Fax: 618/566-7518

- **Store Hours:** Monday-Friday: 8:30-4:30.

- **Secondary Market Lines:** The Morgan Co. specializes in limited edition and retired sports collectibles. The lines include figurines and plates by Salvino, Gartlan USA, Hackett American, and Sports Impressions. The Morgan Co. has recently added limited edition sports magazines to its lines. These include, *Legends, Investor Journal, Cartwrights, Showcase, Ball Street Journal,* and *Sports Card News.*

- **Secondary Market Terms:** Buy-Sell market in sports figurines, plates, and magazines. All trade offers considered. A newly installed computer program matches buyers and sellers. Collector requests will be entered in their nationwide search service.

- **Business History:** The Morgan Co. began specializing in limited edition figurines and plates in 1988 after the first two Gartlan figurines (Rose and Schmidt) and the first Sports Impression figurine (Mattingly) were already sold out. When *Legends* began publication in 1988, the Morgan Co. was one of the original distributors. The Morgan Co. publishes illustrated catalogs on limited edition sports collectibles and limited edition sports magazines. The regular cost is $3.00 each; however, either or both will be sent free if collectors mention that they saw the listing in this directory-- *The Directory toSecondary Market Retailers* with their request.

• • • • • • •

Morris Antiques

2716 Flintlock Drive
Henderson, KY 42420
Phone: 502/826-8378

- **Hours:** Monday–Saturday: 9:00-9:00. By appointment only.

- **Secondary Market Lines:** Hallmark.

- **Secondary Market Terms:** No consignments. Buy outright.

- **Business History:** Allen and Pat Morris have owned their mail order business since 1970 and have been active in the secondary market for twenty years. The couple became active in the Hallmark secondary market in 1983.

  Morris Antiques carries Hallmark ornaments dating from 1973 through the current year. The firm provides a 26-page price list to interested parties. Call for details. The Morrises exhibit at the Stewart shows at the Kentucky State Fair Grounds in Louisville and various other shows throughout the country. They also appear at open houses in Hallmark stores in Kentucky and Indiana.

• • • • • • •

Morton's Antique & Estate Jewelry

533 Parkway
Gatlinburg, TN 37738
Phone: 615/436-7386

- **Store Hours:** Daily: 9:00-11:00p.m.

- **Secondary Market Lines:** Emmett Kelly, Jr., Duncan Royale, Norman Rockwell, Ron Lee, Raikes Bears, Jan Hagara, Maud Humphrey.

- **Secondary Market Terms:** Consignment: 20%. Buy outright. Call for details.

- **Business History:** Morton's is a family-owned operation, in business since 1969. The company's goal is customer satisfaction with a personal touch. Members of the Ward family personally contact their customers by phone to inform them of the availability of secondary market pieces. The store also hosts several special events and artist appearances throughout the year.

• • • • • • •

MSdataBase Solutions

4635 Oak Creek Drive
Fort Wayne, IN 46835
Phone: 219/486-6152

- **Hours:** Daily: 9:00-11:00pm-order/information. 6:00pm-11:00pm: technical support.

- **Secondary Market Lines:** Precious Moments and other collectibles.

- **Business History:** MSdataBase Solutions provides computer software to maintain a complete inventory for insurance purposes and secondary market updates. This "user friendly" program can provide reports on any number of areas including insurance, inventory value changes, in addition to customized reports. Also, collectors can find and search for information immediately.

  Michael and Suzanne Belofsky formed MSdataBase Solutions in 1991. The first program introduced by the firm was the Collectibles DataBase, which is an all-purpose program, tailored for collectors who wish to keep an inventory of everything they own -- excellent for insurance purposes. This program does not contain a price guide.

  MSdataBase Solutions also makes available the Collectibles DataBase for Precious Moments collectors. This innovative program comes with a Precious Collectibles Price Guide Data Disk. Updates can be purchased yearly. Collectors' and dealers' versions are available. All programs offered by MSdataBase Solutions are easy to use, with technical support available at no charge. Interested collectors are invited to call or write for a flyer and additional information.

• • • • • • •

Natalia's Collectibles

19949-130th NE
Woodinville, WA 98072
Phone: 206/481-4575

Natalia's Collectibles
Limited Edition Plates, Figurines, Dolls
Gifts For All Occasions

- **Store Hours:** Tuesday–Saturday: 10:00-7:00.

- **Secondary Market Lines:** Ashton-Drake dolls, Sarah's Attic, Jan Hagara, Maud Humphrey, Thomas Kinkade, and all limited edition plates.

- **Secondary Market Terms:** Consignments and buy outright.

- **Business History:** Natalia's Collectibles was established as a small store in a quiet garden-type surrounding in 1982. Originally dealing only in limited edition plates on the primary market, the firm soon established themselves in the secondary market for plates. Likewise, as dolls and figurines were added to the store, they assisted their clients with a secondary market outlet.

  As a Bradford Exchange and NALED member, Natalia's Collectibles is dedicated to friendly expert service in both the primary and secondary markets.

New England Collectibles Exchange

201 Pine Avenue
Clarksburg, MA 01247
Phone: 413/663-3643
Phone: 800/854-6323

NEW ENGLAND
COLLECTIBLES EXCHANGE
BROKER OF FINE COLLECTIBLES
GNOMES ◆ FIGURINES ◆ COTTAGES

- **Store Hours:** Monday–Friday: 2:00-9:00. Anytime Saturday or messages can be left anytime; calls returned promptly.

- **Secondary Market Lines:** Tom Clark, David Winter, Gregory Perillo, Tim Wolfe, Maurice Wideman, Marty Bell. Will also broker depending on members' need: Kuck, Precious Moments, Hummel, Chilmark, Department 56, lithographs and more.

- **Secondary Market Terms:** Collectibles are listed free for active members. Members pay $16.00 annually. Newsletters are published eight to ten times a year. Collectors may list buy, sell or trade items. Newsletters include what's hot in listed artists, retired pieces, low edition numbered pieces, as well as special interest pieces, a "wanted to buy" column and a schedule of where to meet artists "on tour." Buyers pay a 15% commission (or a $5 minimum) plus shipping costs from the Exchange to their door. Serving individuals and dealers.

- **Business History:** An active collector of several artists, Bob Dorman developed the New England Collectibles Exchange (NECE) with the rules of honest, fair, courteous and confidential personal service to all buyers and sellers. NECE is service-oriented; members supply the collectibles and NECE markets them. NECE will ship collectibles insured to collectors worldwide.

OHI Exchange

1600 River Road
New Braunfels, TX 78132
Phone: 800/627-1600
Fax: 512/629-0153

- **Store Hours:** Monday–Friday: 9:00-6:00. Saturday: 9:30-6:00. Sundays: Closed.

- **Secondary Market Lines:** ANRI, Boehm, Chilmark, Cybis, David Winter, DeGrazia, Department 56, dolls, Duncan Royale, Emmett Kelly Jr., Goebel, Goebel/Olszewski, Hummel, Jan Hagara, June McKenna, Krystonia, Lilliput Lane, Lladro, Lowell Davis, Malcolm Cooper, Miss Martha's Originals (All God's Children), Maud Humphrey, McClelland, Memories of Yesterday, Norman Rockwell, OHI steins, Perillo, Precious Moments, Raikes, Ricker-Bartlett, Royal Doulton, Sarah's Attic, Sports issues, Steiff, steins, Swarovski, Tom Clark, Wee Forest Folk, Zolan.

- **Secondary Market Terms:** Commission sales matching buyers and sellers. Lowest available price always quoted. All merchandise inspected. Buyer has return privilege. Call for sample packet with details and complimentary newsletter, if available.

- **Business History:** The OHI Exchange, a division of Opa's Haus Inc., deals with a broad spectrum of retired collectibles on a daily basis. Supported by a bi-monthly newsletter ($19.00 annually with free binder), The Exchange works to maintain an impeccable reputation for service and fair treatment. The Exchange is one of three primary divisions of Opa's Haus Inc. The company also operates a wholesale division featuring collectible steins it produces and a retail division encompassing four Texas stores.

The Old Miller Place

21358 Highway 99 E.
Aurora, OR 97002
Phone: 503/678-1128
Fax: 503/263-8948

- **Store Hours:** Tuesday-Sat.: 11:00-5:00. Sunday: 12:00-5:00.

- **Secondary Market Lines:** Duncan Royale, Chilmark, Middleton, M.I. Hummel, Bing & Grondahl and Royal Copenhagen plates, Steiff, Raikes, Vanderbears, Old World Christmas lights.

- **Secondary Market Terms:** Buy outright. Consignment: 35%. Locator service. Some trade.

- **Business History:** The Old Miller Place is aptly named, in that this store was originally built in 1892 by the Miller family, many of whom lived there until 1978. Dick and Diane Anderson purchased the store from its previous owners, who had opened a collectibles store in this tourist town of 300. Diane, an antique collector, felt that she had found the perfect job, combining her enjoyment of people with her love for collecting. The Old Miller Place is a Showcase Dealer for Chilmark, in addition to housing one of the largest displays of Duncan Royale in Oregon. In fact, the previous owner had collected Santas, and Diane continued the tradition of displaying 600 Santas, from turn-of-the-century to present day. The Santas are shown on the staircase November 1 through January. A special event is held in the fall, featuring sales reps from various manufacturers. Collectors visiting Miller's will be warmly greeted with a hot cup of coffee and given a tour of this historical house, with time to browse through this fascinating store!

The Ornament Connection

512 East Riverside Drive #104
Austin, TX 78704
Phone: 512/441-7133
Fax: 512/441-1918

- **Store Hours:** Mail order or by appointment only.

- **Secondary Market Lines:** Enesco, Hallmark, Carlton.

- **Secondary Market Terms:** Buy outright.

- **Business History:** The Ornament Connection has been selling collectible Christmas ornaments by mail since 1987. Sammie Gayle Dwyer is the owner whose own passion for collecting ornaments became a business of finding ornaments for other collectors.

  Thousands of ornaments make up the ever-changing inventory. Sammie buys, sells and even occasionally trades ornaments with collectors. Orders are guaranteed and can be returned in seven days refund or replacement.

Osterville Newstand

3 Wianno Avenue
Osterville, MA 02655
Phone: 508/428-2151

- **Store Hours:** Monday–Friday: 5:30-5:30. Sunday: 5:30-1:00.

- **Secondary Market Lines:** June McKenna, Inc.

- **Secondary Market Terms:** Buy outright.

- **Business History:** Osterville Newstand has been in business for 100 years. Owners Neil and Barbara Perkins purchased the firm in 1981. At that time, the business, located in a small town on Cape Cod, included a newstand and an old-fashioned soda fountain. They changed the scope of the business to include collectibles. Today, the Perkins feature several specialty lines, including June McKenna, Byers' Choice, Department 56, David Winter, Lowell Davis, Goebel Miniatures, Chilmark and a fine line of hand-carved birds.

  Open houses are an important part of Osterville Newstand's annual promotions. Artist June McKenna makes personal appearances at the store. Yearly Christmas open houses are also organized in conjunction with other area businesses, complete with food and singing.

• • • • • • •

Our Place-
A General Store

North Side of Square
P.O. Box 234
Lynchburg, TN 37352
Phone: 615/759-4411

• **Store Hours:** Daily: 9:30-5:30.

• **Secondary Market Lines:** Cairn Studio:Tom Clark Creations; Miss Martha's Originals, All God's Children, Hamilton Gifts: Maud Humphrey; Sarah's Attic: Black Heritage and Angels.

• **Secondary Market Terms:** No consignments.They attempt to locate pieces for buyers or match buyers with sellers. They have numerous retired pieces for sale. Call for information on their selection and prices.

• **Business History:** Our Place has been in business since 1982, offering a broad range of gifts in addition to their limited edition collectible lines. Limited edition collectibles are shipped free within the continental U.S. Most items/orders will be processed immediately for next day shipping. The store offers friendly, knowledgeable service. They will gladly recommend other sources of help in any area of service they cannot fill.

Papillon Ltd.

Fitgers on the Lake
600 E. Superior
Duluth, MN 55802
Phone: 218/726-0308

- **Store Hours:** Monday–Saturday: 10:00-9:00. Sunday: 11:00-5:00.

- **Secondary Market Lines:** Bradford plates, ANRI figurines and dolls, Chilmark, Hudson Pewter, Hamilton plates, Perillo, Lowell Davis, M.I. Hummel, Tom Clark, David Winter, Lilliput Lane, Royal Doulton, Swarovski, Kaiser, Emmett Kelly, Jr., PenDelfin, Ashton-Drake, Lexington Hall dolls, Wee Forest Folk, Bing & Grondahl dolls, plates and figurines, Royal Copenhagen plates and figurines, Maruri, Roman and NAO figurines by Lladro.

- **Secondary Market Terms:** Locator service.

- **Business History:** Mother-daughter team, Thelma and Gay Lynne Liebertz, opened Papillon in 1984. Prior to this, these collectors-turned-business owners operated a restaurant and collectibles gift shop in a canoe resort area on the Gunflint Trail for several years. They bring a great deal of experience into the business, as they are considered to be one of the largest plate dealers in northern Minnesota. Papillon is a Redemption Center for Chilmark, Hudson, Emmett Kelly, Jr., Lowell Davis, M.I. Hummel, ANRI, Tom Clark, David Winter, Lilliput Lane, Royal Doulton, Swarovski and PenDelfin. The Liebertzs have hosted many artist appearances, including prominent plate artists, Royal Doulton and Lilliput Lane painters and ANRI Woodcarvers.

The Plate Niche

14 Annapolis St.
Annapolis, MD 21401
Phone: 410/268-5106
Phone: 800/659-6808

The Plate Niche

- **Store Hours:** Tuesday-Saturday: 10:00-5:00.

- **Secondary Market Lines:** All plates, Ashton-Drake dolls, Hamilton Heritage dolls, Sports memorabilia: Sports Impressions, Gartlan USA, Pro Sport.

- **Secondary Market Terms:** Locator service: specializes in finding plates, sports memorabilia and dolls.

- **Business History:** Plate Niche owner, Lorraine Zublionis, began her business in 1990. An art lover, she took an affinity to collector plates and never looked back! Discovering a demand for a plate dealer in her area, Lorraine responded by opening her shop, and today, carries plates and more! Collectors began calling Lorraine, looking for older collector plates, and eventually her secondary market business expanded into a very busy sideline. She enjoys the thrill of the hunt, as she seeks back plate issues and other retired collectibles.

  An authorized Bradford plate dealer, The Plate Niche hosts open houses and special events annually. Collectors doing business with this store will also be placed on a mailing list to receive postcards with product announcements, newsletters and catalogs.

• • • • • • •

Prestige Collections

The Mall at Short Hills
Short Hills, NJ 07078
Phone: 201/376-3537
Phone: Orders only: 800/227-7979
Fax: 201/376-7919

- **Store Hours:** Monday–Friday: 10:00-9:00.
  Saturday: 10:00-6:00. Sunday: 12:00-5:00.

- **Secondary Market Lines:** Lladro, M.I. Hummel,
  Armani, David Winter, Lalique, Swarovski, Caithness, Daum.

- **Secondary Market Terms:** No consignments.
  Buy/sell match service.

- **Business History:** Located in one of the finest malls in
  the state of New Jersey, Prestige Collections is a service-
  oriented store that carries fine gifts and collectibles -- one of
  the only collectible stores in the area.

  Established in 1977, Prestige Collections is a Redemption
  Center for the lines listed above. Owners, Florian and
  Clyde, offer collectors the opportunity to purchase specialty
  pieces active on the secondary market, including collector
  club exclusives and hard-to-locate collectibles and limited
  edition pieces. They run many artist and manufacturer-
  sponsored shows at the store and mail several catalogs and
  other pertinent information throughout the year. They ship
  anywhere in the U.S.A.

• • • • • • •

Quality Collectables

71 S. Mast Street
Goffstown, NH 03045
Phone: 603/497-4721
Phone: 800/422-6514

- **Hours:** Daily: 9:00am-10:00pm.

- **Secondary Market Lines:** Gartlan USA, Salvino, Pro Sport Creations, Sports Impressions, Sport Porcelain, Sports Collectors Warehouse, Pro Sport Images, Delgado Studios, Hartland Figurines, Authentic Impressions.

- **Secondary Market Terms:** Consignments. Buy outright and trades. Convenient layaway plans available.

- **Business History:** As a kid, Matt Moyer collected baseball cards and sports related items -- and never stopped! Today, he is the owner of a successful mail order business, selling sports collectibles on both the primary and secondary market.

  In business since 1988 and one of the largest sports art dealers on the east coast, Quality Collectables is a Redemption Center for Gartlan USA, Sports Impressions and Salvino collector clubs. Newsletters are published every six to eight weeks and are free to customers. Other collectors may order an annual subscription for $10.00.

• • • • • • •

Larry Rager's
Gifts of Perfection

11309 Kramer Drive
Evansville, IN 47712
Phone: 812/985-2962

𝔇𝔦𝔠𝔨𝔢𝔫'𝔰 𝔙𝔦𝔩𝔩𝔞𝔤𝔢

"COLLECTOR"

- **Hours :** Consulting, buying, selling and trading by phone until midnight.

- **Secondary Market Lines:** Department 56: Dickens, Christmas in the City, New England, Snow Village, Alpine, Home Town Series, Williamsburg, Victorian, Snowbabies.

- **Secondary Market Terms:** Buy-sell-trade. Appraisals are available. Call for details.

- **Business History:** Larry Rager refers to himself as "your friendly Department 56 secondary market dealer and consultant," agreed upon by the many collectors and dealers who have had the opportunity to converse with Larry! Having collected Department 56 since 1986, Larry started buying, selling and trading houses in 1987. The pieces are insured and shipped U.P.S. and are fully guaranteed. Larry conducts his secondary market business by phone and at shows nationwide, including the South Bend Collectibles Exposition, Bachman's Gathering and the Xmas Faire in Gatlinburg. Larry has conducted seminars since 1989, speaking to dealers and Department 56 clubs. Topics range from tips on the secondary market and insuring your collection, to variances of Department 56 pieces, displaying a collection and more. The "Kneer Purrfec" restoration process is employed by Larry to restore Department 56 pieces for collectors whose houses require some tender loving care. Call for details.

Rainbow's End

901 Milford Church Road Suite G
Marietta , GA 30060
Phone: 404/431-0950

- **Store Hours:** Monday–Friday: 10:30-6:00. Saturday: 10:00-5:00.

- **Secondary Market Lines:** Original Appalachian Artwork, All God's Children, Raikes Bears, Madame Alexander Dolls.

- **Secondary Market Terms:** Consignments. Buy outright. Layaways. Trades.

- **Business History:** Jean Wallace was a doll collector who happened to meet Cabbage Patch trademark creator, Xavier Roberts, when he was just entering the doll market. In order to open an official adoption center, Jean was able to work out an agreement with a friend in an art gallery -- a gallery which she eventually took over in 1979 and changed gradually to a collectibles store. Jean's dolls are all displayed in realistic settings, such as cribs and highchairs.

Rainbow's End provides price lists and appraisals for All God's Children figurines and the beloved Cabbage Patch Kids. Artist signings and an open house are held once annually. The store is a Redemption Center for Maud Humphrey, All God's Children, Attic Babies and Cabbage Patch Kids.

Robinette's Gift Barn

3142 Four Mile Road NE
Grand Rapids, MI 49505
Phone: 616/361-7180
Phone: 800/GFT-BARN
Fax: 616/361-6445

- **Store Hours:** Monday–Saturday: 10:00-5:00. Sunday: 1:00-5:00, September-February.

- **Secondary Market Lines:** Department 56: Heritage and Snow Villages, Snowbabies; Sarah's Attic, Legends, David Winter, Lilliput Lane, Cat's Meow.

- **Secondary Market Terms:** Consignment. Commission varies on the collectible. Seller pays commission.

- **Business History:** An authentic 106-year-old farm is the setting for Robinette's Apple Haus & Gift Barn. Robinette's is an orchard, where apple cider is freshly pressed from Labor Day to spring, while the Country Gift Barn welcomes collectors to browse through a charming 6,000 square foot gift store that resembles the country general stores of old. Visitors will enjoy the fine gifts, collectibles and home decor on display in this inviting atmosphere.

  In business since 1986, Robinette's Gift Barn carries line after line of collectibles. Their knowledgeable staff is on hand to assist collectors who have questions about their hobby. The store is a Club Redemption Center for many of the firms listed above and hosts many open houses and special events each year.

• • • • • • •

Rochelle's Fine Gifts

Franklin Park Mall
Toledo, OH 43623
Phone: 419/472-7673
Phone: 800/458-6585

- **Store Hours:** Monday–Saturday: 10:00-9:00. Sunday: 12:00-5:00.

- **Secondary Market Lines:** Precious Moments, David Winter, Bradford plates, Maud Humphrey, Department 56: Christmas in the City, New England, Dickens, Snow Village, Village accessories.

- **Secondary Market Terms:** Buy outright. Call for details.

- **Business History:** Rochelle's Fine Gifts opened its doors in 1977 in one of Toledo's largest and best fashion malls. The mall is also the site for the annual International Doll and Teddy Bear Show.

  Owner, Rochelle Pfaff, covers the secondary market for all of the lines listed above and is open to consider other retired items as well.

  Rochelle's is a member of NALED and the only plate dealer in Toledo. The firm is a Showcase Dealer for Department 56 and is one of the largest dealers in northwestern Ohio for Precious Moments. The store is also a Redemption Center for Maud Humphrey, David Winter and Precious Moments collectors clubs. Rochelle's hosts occasional open houses and offers free gift-wrapping.

Rose Marie's

1119 Lincoln Avenue
Evansville, IN 47714
Phone: 812/423-7557
Phone: 800/637-5734
Fax: 812/423-7578

- **Store Hours:** Monday–Thursday: 10:00-5:00, Friday: 10:00-7:00. Saturday: 10:00-5:00.

- **Secondary Market Lines:** Department 56 and M. I. Hummel.

- **Secondary Market Terms:** Rose Marie's secondary market works for the collector – whether it's the buyer or the seller. They will help collectors locate the piece they're looking for. Listed price plus 10%. Fully guaranteed. Call for details.

- **Business History:** Rose Marie's was founded in 1958 by Rose Marie Hillenbrand. Looking for a way to aid her missionary sons in Guatamala and on the Indian reservations of the Black Hills, Rose Marie began by selling a few exquisite pieces from a restored wardrobe in her living room. Today, over 30 years later, Rose Marie's specializes in assisting the collector in gift giving and the acquisition of fine collectibles. The store services and supports 27 collector clubs and does an average of 10 promotions and artist shows a year, on and off Rose Marie's premises.

  After 33 years, Rose Marie's dream was fulfilled when her son, Bill, purchased a historical home, which became the new 'old' home of Rose Marie's! This move was celebrated with a grand opening in June of 1991.

Rossmyer Gallery

1200 E. Alosta Ste. 110
Glendora, CA 91740
Phone: 818/914-1611

Rossmyer Gallery

- **Store Hours:** Monday–Friday: 10:00-5:30. Saturday: 10:00-4:00.

- **Secondary Market Lines:** David Winter, Lladro, Swarovski, M.I. Hummel, All God's Children, Jan Hagara, Maud Humphrey, Dolls: A. Himstedt, Ashton-Drake, Gadco; Lithographs: F. Stone, T. Kinkade, Oz Franca, Maija, Zolan, S. Kuck.

- **Secondary Market Terms:** No consignments. Buy outright.

- **Business History:** Rossmyer Gallery has been in business since 1978, placing emphasis on service to individual customers. They handle all major collectibles and specialize in finding sold out and hard-to-find collectibles.

Rostand Fine Jewelers

8349 Foothill Blvd.
Sunland, CA 91040
Phone: 818/352-7814
Phone: 800/222-9208

- **Store Hours:** Monday–Friday: 9:30-6:00. Saturday: 9:30-5:30. Closed Sundays except in December.

- **Secondary Market Lines:** Lladro, Swarovski, Lalique, David Winter Cottages, Armani, Ron Lee Clowns, Chilmark, M.I. Hummel, Walt Disney Classics Collection.

- **Secondary Market Terms:** Buy outright. Consignment with commission on sale.

- **Business History:** Rostand Fine Jewelers has been established in Sunland, California, a suburb of Los Angeles, for 32 years. Herb Rostand is internationally recognized as an authority on Lladro art and is considered by the Lladro organization to be "the pioneer of the Lladro secondary market." Rostand Jewelers houses one of the largest collections of Lladro porcelains, estimated to exceed 2,500 pieces. Herb Rostand provides collectors with expert appraisals for estate evaluation, insurance replacements and individual collection records.

  The Rostand Annual Lladro Auction and Festival, held in Los Angeles, is enjoyed by some 1,500 Lladro afficiandos from the United States and all over the world. Collectors attend seminars, experience the excitement of the auction and the camaraderie of new found fellow Lladro collectors on a day devoted exclusively to the world of Lladro art.

Rystad's Limited Editions

1013 Lincoln Avenue
San Jose, CA 95125
Phone: 408/279-1960

- **Store Hours:** Tuesday-Saturday: 10:00-5:00. Can be reached off-hours via answering machine.

- **Secondary Market Lines:** Red Skelton, Rockwell, Lladro, M.I. Hummel, David Winter, Wee Forest Folk, Ashton-Drake, Donald Zolan, ornaments: Lenox, Enesco Treasury and Gorham; All God's Children, Goebel Miniatures, Duncan Royale, Department 56: Snowbabies; Raikes Bears, Disney, Royal Copenhagen, Bing & Grondahl, Miss Martha Originals, Rockwell, Thomas Kinkade graphics, all plates.

- **Secondary Market Terms:** Consignments. Buy out-right. Buy/sell brokerage. Call for details.

- **Business History:** Dean Rystad started in the collectibles mail order business in 1967, while he was still teaching business. In 1978, Rystad opened a store, which today features 85 percent collector plates. In fact, it's "floor to ceiling" plates, as the store showcases more than 3,000 plates at any given time! Collectors are notified by either phone or mail when their next in a series is available. Rystad's specialty is in locating back issues of collectibles. His track record is about 98 percent on requests. He also offers an appraisal service. Rystad's is a Redemption Center for Precious Moments, Memories of Yesterday, M.I. Hummel, All God's Children, Maud Humphrey, David Winter, Lilliput Lane and most other collector clubs.

St. Nicks

5221 S. Santa Fe Dr.
Littleton, CO 80120
Phone: 303/798-8087
Phone: 800/875-8865
Fax: 303/798-2450

- **Store Hours:** Monday-Saturday: 10:00-6:00.

- **Secondary Market Lines:** Department 56: all villages and accessories, cold casts, light-ups, Snowbabies, no snow-globes; Lilliput Lane, David Winter, M.I. Hummel.

- **Secondary Market Terms:** 25% commission. Occasionally buys outright. Buy/sell brokerage available for most collectibles.

- **Business History:** As Colorado's largest Christmas store, St. Nick's has been in business since 1975. Collectors seeking an extensive selection of yuletide collectibles will truly enjoy a walk through eleven rooms of Christmas!

  St. Nicks is a Redemption Center for Precious Moments and M.I. Hummel collector clubs and is also a Showcase Dealer for Department 56. Sue Sealy and her staff host an open house annually during the first week in November. Customers will receive periodic mailings and newsletters and also are given incentives when they purchase collectibles at this very festive store. Call for details.

  St. Nick's maintains an up-to-date record of retired collectibles available. Interested individuals should send a self-addressed stamped envelope for the current listing. This store is also a member of the Gift Creations Catalog.

• • • • • • •

Sam's Steins & Collectibles

2207 Lincoln Highway East (Rt. 30)
Lancaster, PA 17602
Phone: 717/394-6404

SAM'S
STEINS & COLLECTIBLES

- **Store Hours:** Monday- Wednesday, Saturday: 10:00-6:00.
  Thursday, Friday, 10:00-8:00. Sunday: 12:00-5:00. Closed:
  Mondays October-May. Sundays Jan.-May.

- **Secondary Market Lines:** Beer steins: Anheuser-Busch,
  Miller, Coors, Strohs, Pabst, Hamm's, Heileman, Yuengling,
  also large selection of German beer steins.

- **Secondary Market Terms:** Buy outright.

- **Business History:** A collector himself, owner Sam May
  houses one of the largest displays of beer memorabilia in the
  United States. Over 500 different U.S. and German steins are
  on display at Sam's Steins and Collectibles.

  The company has been in business since 1971 and specializes in brewery advertising items such as steins, neons,
  signs, tap markers and mirrors. Sam also carries Legends,
  Ande Rooney Porcelain signs, whiskey decanters and Lledo
  and ERTL trucks.

Saville's Limited Editions

Northway Mall #2174 8000 McKnight Rd.
Pittsburgh, PA 15237
Phone: 412/366-5458
Fax: 412/369-9524

- **Store Hours:** Monday–Saturday: 10:00-9:00. Sunday: 12:00-5:00.

- **Secondary Market Lines:** Department 56: All Villages, Snowbabies, accessories and cold cast; M.I. Hummel, Precious Moments, David Winter, Emmett Kelly, Jr., Lilliput Lane, Memories of Yesterday, Ashton-Drake dolls, Tom Clark, June McKenna, Chilmark, Swarovski, Annalee, Byers' Choice, Maud Humphrey, Bradford plates, Wee Forest Folk, Lowell Davis.

- **Secondary Market Terms:** Buy/sell outright. Locator service.

- **Business History:** Mayne Saville opened Saville's in 1981, making customer service her top priority. Her family has been in the retail business since the 1800s, therefore Mayne knows the importance of maintaining a staff that is fully trained to assist and educate the collector. The store carries a complete line of the many products featured, including extensive displays of Department 56 and Precious Moments. Saville's is a Redemption Center for over twenty collector clubs. A member of NALED and Gift Creations Concepts, this store has hosted several artist appearances, welcoming Lowell Davis, Bob Olszewski, Tom Clark, Emmett Kelly, Jr., artisans from John Hine Studios and M.I. Hummel.

Secondary Collectible Service

1656 E. Garfield Road
New Springfield, OH 44443
Phone: 216/549-9479
Phone: 800/862-2030

- **Store Hours:** Call 24 hours daily.

- **Secondary Market Lines:** M.I. Hummel, Department 56:Villages and Snowbabies; Lladro, Swarovski, Rockwell, Precious Moments, Goebel, Schmid, Disney, Gorham dolls, ANRI, Lowell Davis, Royal Doulton, Duncan Royale, Emmett Kelly, Jr., David Winter, Lilliput Lane, June McKenna, Tom Clark Gnomes.

- **Secondary Market Terms:** This business is a buy/sell brokerage. When availability of a collectible has been confirmed, the buyer sends a check or money order to Secondary Collectible Service. Concurrently, the seller ships the item to Secondary Collectible Service for a quick, but thorough inspection. At the time of shipping, a notice is mailed to the buyer. If the firm does not hear from the buyer within a week, they will assume that the party is happy with the item, and the payment will then be sent to the seller. At this point, there can be no returns or refunds. Their charge: 20% plus shipping and handling.

- **Business History:** Secondary Collectible Service offers over a quarter of a century of experience in fine collectibles and limited editions. They are recommended by the famous Hummel Gift Shop in New Springfield, Ohio and are recognized by most major manufacturers and factories.

The Second Step

6234 Mojave Drive
San Jose, CA 95120
Phone: 408/927-9745
Phone: 800/231-9055

THE SECOND STEP
Lladró Secondary Market
6234 Mojave Drive San Jose, CA 95120

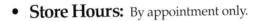

- **Store Hours:** By appointment only.

- **Secondary Market Lines:** Lladro

- **Secondary Market Terms:** Provides a listing service. Commission varies. Call for details.

- **Business History:** The Second Step is a relatively new business designed to provide a "search and find" and listing service to collectors of Lladro. Owners Doris and Bud Serpa started out as Lladro collectors. Eventually, they decided to sell a few of their figurines on the secondary market and discovered there was a need for a secondary market outlet in their area.

  The Serpas are able to answer a wide variety of questions on Lladro collectibles, utilizing their computerized databases and reference library. They can assist collectors in identifying the pieces they own, sometimes over the phone without a name or model number! Their service-oriented firm is in full operation, matching buyers with sellers. Their current price list contains over 280 pieces, offering many retired pieces as well as special incentives on non-retired pieces.

  "The Second Step -- Notes" newsletter is printed quarterly and includes Lladro product news and an updated price list. Collectors are invited to call if they would care to be placed on the mailing list.

• • • • • • •

Serendipity

5500 Greenville Ave.
1203 Old Town
Dallas, TX 75206
Phone: 214/692-0249   *Serendipity*
Phone: 800/767-4027
Fax: 214/692-5773

• **Store Hours:** Monday–Saturday: 10:00-6:00.

• **Secondary Market Lines:** David Winter, Lowell Davis,
M.I. Hummel, Lladro, ANRI, Lalique, Royal Doulton,
Swarovski, Chilmark, plates, Olszewski Miniatures, Boehm,
Russian Lacquer.

• **Secondary Market Terms:** Some consignments. Buy
outright. Layaways available.

• **Business History:** Imagine 10,000 square feet of collectibles, and you've seen Serendipity, one of the largest collectibles retailers in the country. Collectors themselves,
owners Eveline and Galen Kirkland have owned Serendipity
since 1971, specializing in service and special orders. Since
the facility is so large, the Kirklands are able to stock entire
collections of many lines simultaneously -- and still have
room to add new releases! The couple hosts many open
houses and artist appearances and offers appraisal services.
Serendipity is a Redemption Center for the lines listed
above. Attractive and informative newsletters are mailed
periodically. Interested collectors should call to add their
names to the store's mailing list.

• • • • • • •

Shanfields-Meyers

188 Oullette Avenue
Windsor, Ontario N9A 1A4
Phone: (Canada) 519/252-9702
Phone: (US) 313/961-1966 or 961-8435
Fax: 519/253-3355

- **Store Hours:** Monday–Wednesday: 9:00-6:00. Thursday-Friday: 9:00-9:00. Saturday: 9:00-6:00. Sunday: 10:00-6:00.

- **Secondary Market Lines:** Precious Moments, M. I. Hummel, Lladro, Royal Doulton, Swarovski, Armani, ANRI, Wedgwood, Rockwell, Boehm, Gorham, Waterford, Belleek, Orrefors, Reed & Barton, Bing & Grondahl, Kaiser, Caithness, Haviland, Rosenthal, Rorstrand, Royal Worcester, Lalique Spode, Pendelfin, Ispanky, Hutschenreuther, old plates and much, much more!

- **Secondary Market Terms:** No consignment. Buy out-right. Will consider purchasing complete collections. Buy/sell locator service.

- **Business History:** Located just over the U.S. border, two minutes from the Detroit tunnel, Shanfields-Meyers is a treasure trove for those collectors who are looking for a store to browse the whole day long! Founded in 1932, owners Jack and Lina Shanfield stock tens of thousands of old plates and figurines. They specialize in locating hard-to-find collectibles and offer an appraisal service as well. They are a Redemption Center for Swarovski, M.I. Hummel, Lladro, ANRI, Belleek and Royal Doulton collector clubs. This store also sells antique jewelry, discontinued dinnerware, crystal and silverware, including sterling.

The Ship's Bell

105 E. 6th Avenue
Helena, MT 59601
Phone: 406/443-4470

- **Store Hours:** Monday–Friday: 10:00-5:30. Saturday: 11:00-4:00.

- **Secondary Market Lines:** M.I. Hummel, Reco, Hamilton, Bradford plates, Ernst, Villeroy & Boch, Christian Bell, Lowell Davis, Ashton-Drake, Perillo, Redlin, Rockwell, Winton-Roland and more!

- **Secondary Market Terms:** No consignments. Call for details.

- **Business History:** Established in 1973, The Ship's Bell is an authorized Bradford dealer that features a very large plate gallery, in addition to other collectible lines. They are secondary market specialists for the lines listed above and welcome all other inquiries as well. Shirley DeWolf and her staff pride themselves on adding a personal touch, as they work with each and every collector.

• • • • • • •

Shirley's Collectibles-
"Hoosier Happening"

307 E. Main Street
Fowler, IN 47944
Phone: 317/884-0798

- **Store Hours:** Daily: 9:00-9:00.

- **Secondary Market Lines:** Hallmark and Schmid
  ornaments and other Hallmark collectibles.

- **Secondary Market Terms:** Buy outright.
  Layaway available. Call for details.

- **Business History:** In 1983, Shirlet Glotzbach opened
  Shirley's Collectibles, a mail order business, carrying
  Hallmark ornaments and various Hallmark collectibles.
  Shirley's has a complete selection of ornaments in stock, dating back from 1973 to the current year. She became known
  as an ornament expert and began receiving such a tremen-
  dous amount of correspondence, that she found it increasingly difficult to answer collectors' questions personally. In
  response to this enthusiastic demand for information,
  Shirley initiated the "Hoosier Happening," an informative
  newsletter with a personal touch. Newsletters are published
  five times annually, with subscriptions costing $3.50 when
  accompanied with an order, or $10.00 without an order.
  Each issue of "Hoosier Happening" includes personal notes,
  fascinating articles on ornament collecting, new product
  information and "what's hot." A 16-page price list is included with each issue.

Sier's Secondary Exchange

8609 10th Avenue SE
Everett,WA 98208
Phone: 800/659-7796

- **Business Hours:** Monday–Saturday: 8:00-10:00.

- **Secondary Market Lines:** Department 56, David Winter, Lilliput Lane, Lladro, Swarovski, M.I. Hummel, All God's Children, Emmett Kelly, Jr., Chilmark, Goebel Miniatures, Lowell Davis, Jan Hagara, Krystonia, Hallmark, ANRI, Tom Clark Gnomes, Wee Forest Folk, Precious Moments, dolls, plates, prints and more.

- **Secondary Market Terms:** Buy/sell brokerage. Sliding commission scale, as low as 5%. Call for details. Sier's buys some pieces outright.

- **Business History:** Maria Sier began collecting Department 56 in 1987. Her husband Tim, a licensed mutual fund and insurance salesman, was amazed at the appreciation of the pieces over the years. In 1991, the couple's hobby turned into a business, as they established Sier's Secondary Exchange, an aftermarket firm for buyers and sellers of retired items. Collectors may list pieces with the exchange at no cost. Buyers' and sellers' names are kept confidential during the entire process. Unique to Sier's is the sliding brokerage commission -- as low as 5%!. The firm also has taken out a $10,000 fidelity bond to protect all parties involved during business transactions. Interested collectors can call Sier's for a price list.

• • • • • • •

Something So Special
Jewelry, Gifts
COLLECTIBLES

Edgebrook Center
1617 N. Alpine Rd.
Rockford, IL 61107
Phone: 815/226-1331

"Rockford's Most Unique Store"

- **Hours:** Monday-Friday: 10:00-8:30. Saturday: 10:00-5:00. Holiday hours: Open Sundays, late October-December.

- **Secondary Market Lines:** Precious Moments, Tom Clark Gnomes, Department 56, Swarovski, David Winter, Lladro, Chilmark, Lilliput Lane, Krystonia, Lowell Davis, M.I. Hummel, Penni-Anne Cross graphics, Bradford plates.

- **Secondary Market Terms:** Some consignments. Buy outright. Buy/sell brokerage.

- **Business History:** Owner Diane Tureson aptly named her store to reflect her own philisophy: she sells 'special' items to customers she treats in a 'special' manner. And that is what this store has been doing since 1980. Members of NALED and Collectors Showcase, Something So Special is a Redemption Center for about 22 collector clubs. They are a Vanguard Dealer for Lladro, a Showcase Dealer for Chilmark, a Blue Ribbon Dealer for Sandicast, a Distinguished Service Retailer for Precious Moments, and an Authorized Dealer for Department 56, and most other collectibles. Something So Special has the first local PM club chapter ever to be formed in the country, recognized by Enesco. This award-winning store hosts many open houses and publishes price lists, catalogs and newsletters. Mail a self-addressed stamped envelope with request. A local newspaper poll voted Something So Special Rockford's 'most unique store.'

Spencer's China & Gallery

3772 Richmond Avenue
Houston, TX 77027
Phone: 800/742-7766
Phone: 713/871-8900
Fax: 713/871-1140

- **Stores Hours:** Monday-Saturday: 10:00-5:00.

- **Secondary Market Lines:** David Winter, Lilliput Lane, Legends, Thomas Kinkade.

- **Secondary Market Terms:** Buy outright. Some consignment.

- **Business History:** Years ago, Pete Lippincott used to buy and sell U.S. gold and silver coins as a hobby. In 1970, Pete took his knowledge of collecting and opened Spencer's, a full-service collectibles store. In 1976, the store began carrying tabletop items, including fine dinnerware. Today, Spencer's offers its customers service, integrity and fair prices. The store is a Redemption Center for M.I. Hummel, Lladro, Lilliput Lane, David Winter and Armani collector clubs. New primary lines include Little Cheezers and the Lincoln County Garden Club figurines. Spencer's publishes a newsletter for interested collectors and Pete will do searches for retired pieces, upon request.

A new Spencer's store was opened in June 1992 at 205 Midway, Old Town Spring, Spring, Texas 77373. Collectors can call the store at 713/355-5059. Store hours are daily from 10:00-5:00.

• • • • • • •

Sports Memorabilia, Etc.

11841 Ventura Blvd.
Studio City, CA 91604   **Est. 1978**
Phone: 818/766-6622
Fax: 818/766-3191

- **Store Hours:** Monday–Saturday: 10:00-6:30. Sunday: 11:00-4:30.

- **Secondary Market Lines:** Gartlan USA, Salvino, Sports Impressions, Hackett American, and older memorabilia, etc.

- **Secondary Market Terms:** Buy, sell and trade.

- **Business History:** Signed sports collectibles have been coveted by sports fans across the country for years. Since 1978, Sports Memorabilia, Etc. has provided "a sports collectors' paradise," where enthusiasts can locate hand-signed plates, figurines, plaques, lithos, sports cards and a large selection of old baseball and sports memorabilia.

  Owner Richard Khoury owns one of the top sports artwork retail establishments in the country. He frequently brings in athletes and artists to sign sports items and to meet collectors. In fact, Khoury specializes in carrying signed sports items, such as signed jerseys and baseballs, as well as baseball cards. Collectors interested in the secondary market can contact Richard with items they wish to sell, or to locate retired pieces.

• • • • • • •

Stacy's Gifts & Collectibles

The Mall at Walpole-Route 1
East Walpole, MA 02032
Phone: 508/668-4212
Phone: 800/STACYS1
Fax: 508/668-7553

- **Store Hours:** Monday–Saturday: 9:30-9:30. Sunday: 12:00-5:00.

- **Secondary Market Lines:** Sebastian, Lladro, Byers' Choice, David Winter, Lilliput Lane, Department 56, Precious Moments, Swarovski, Goebel Miniatures, Lowell Davis, Sports Impressions, Gartlan USA, M.I. Hummel and porcelain dolls.

- **Secondary Market Terms:** Consignments with brokerage fee or outright purchases. Call for information.

- **Business History:** Stacy's Gifts & Collectibles was started by Doris and the late Sherman Edwards in 1973. Over many years of being in the collectible gift business, their customers have come to expect the best. Doris and Sherman were founding members of the Advisory Council of Sebastian Miniatures, and Stacy's remains as active members today. Sherman and Doris were the first to use value ranges to determine secondary market prices. Craig, their son, joined the family business in 1983 and has been instrumental in the development of the store's participation in the secondary market for Lladro, Department 56, sports figurines and plates and David Winter cottages. The Edwards' private collection of Sebastian miniatures has been designated the Official Sebastian Museum and is on permanent display at Stacy's.

The Steinhaus

Miracle Mile Mall
104 17th Avenue NW
Rochester, MN 55901
Phone: 507/280-0132

- **Store Hours:** Monday–Friday: 10:00-9:00. Saturday: 10:00-5:00. Sunday: 12:00-5:00.

- **Secondary Market Lines:** Anheuser-Busch, Miller, Coors, Carolina Collection, Hamms, Pabst, Old Style.

- **Secondary Market Terms:** Locator Service.

- **Business History:** A collector since 1983, Ron Scheid opened The Steinhaus in 1988. The store features a full variety of old and new steins, with an emphasis on Anheuser-Busch. Merchandise is shipped the next day after the order is placed, Monday through Friday.

  The Steinhaus publishes a price list and newsletter three times annually. Collectors are invited to call to be placed on the mailing list.

Stephens-A Touch of Christmas Plus

Plattsburgh Plaza
Plattsburg, NY 12901
Phone: 518/561-5790
Phone: 518/561-4180

- **Store Hours:** Monday–Saturday: 10:00-5:00. Wednesday & Friday: 10:00-9:00.

- **Secondary Market Lines:** Tom Clark Gnomes, June McKenna, Krystonia, Department 56: Dickens, Christmas in the City, Alpine, New England and accessories, Snowbabies, Waterglobes; Cat's Meow, PenDelfin, Annalee, Legends, Niel Rose(Indian Collection), Knot Knoggins, Lee Middleton, Susan Wakeen, United Design, Maruri, Memories of Yesterday.

- **Secondary Market Terms:** Consignments. Some buy outright. Call for details.

- **Business History:** Year-long Christmas collecting is becoming increasingly popular, and Stephens-A Touch of Christmas Plus makes this trend possible by maintaining a year round Christmas shop. A collector since 1977, Steve Duso opened his store in 1985. One of the largest collectible stores in northeastern New York, Stephens carries unique gifts and collectibles from around the world. The store displays and also has available June McKenna figurines and ornaments dating back to her initial releases. An Authorized Dealer for Department 56, Stephens is a Redemption Center for Tom Clark, June McKenna, Krystonia, Cat's Meow, PenDelfin, Annalee, United Design and Memories of Yesterday, and many more. The store also schedules open houses throughout the year.

• • • • • • •

Sterling & Collectables Inc.

P.O. Box 1665
Mansfield, OH 44901
Phone: 800/537-5783
Fax: 419/756-2990

- **Store Hours:** By appointment only, Monday-Friday: 9:00-4:00.

- **Secondary Market Lines:** Gorham, Lunt, Kirk, Towle, Wallace, International, Oneida, Reed & Barton, Cazenovia, Hand & Hammer, Statehouse, Blackington, Stieff, Westmoreland, Easterling, Manchester, Tiffany, Whiting, Dominic & Haff.

- **Secondary Market Terms:** No consignments.

- **Business History:** Sterling & Collectables has been in business for five years, with a combined experience of 25 years in dealing with Christmas ornaments and flatware. They carry back issues in all sterling and most silverplated ornaments. They also specialize in filling in discontinued and obsolete flatware patterns in sterling, silverplate and stainless.

Story Book Kids

STORY BOOK KIDS

3011 Glendale-Milford Rd.
Cincinnati, OH 45241
Phone: 513/769-KIDS
Fax: 513/771-4289

- **Store Hours:** Tuesday-Saturday: 10:00-6:00.

2071 Florence Mall
Florence, KY 41042
Phone: 606/525-7743

- **Store Hours:** Monday-Saturday: 10:00-9:00. Sun: 12:00-6:00

- **Secondary Market Lines:** Cat's Meow, All God's Children, Maud Humphrey, Tom Clark, Precious Moments, Sarah's Attic, Byers' Choice, Department 56, Lilliput Lane, Ray Day, Emmett Kelly, Jr., Snowbabies, United Design.

- **Secondary Market Terms:** Buy outright. No commission.

- **Business History:** Owner Nancy Farrell opened her first Story Book Kids in 1987 in Florence, Kentucky, featuring country gifts and accessories. She soon added collectibles, specializing in Cat's Meow, Tom Clark Gnomes, All God's Children and Sarah's Attic. She now has a second store, in Cincinnati (Evendale), Ohio displaying over 40 complete lines of collectibles and limited editions. The staff at Story Book Kids keeps very busy throughout the year, hosting artist signings and seminars. As a member of NALED, the store distributes a lovely four-color catalog to its mailing list. An appraisal service is also available. Story Book Kids is active in the secondary market, maintaining a customer 'wish list' to match buyers and sellers. Collectors are invited to use their 'No Fee - No Time Frame Layaway Plan' for that special purchase. Collectors should send a self-addressed stamped envelope, telling the firm the lines they collect, and they will send out a current/secondary price list.

• • • • • • •

Swan Galleries, Inc.

1525 E. Park Place Blvd.
Stone Mountain, GA 30087
Phone: 404/498-1324

- **Store Hours:** Monday–Saturday: 10:00-6:00.

- **Secondary Market Lines:** Department 56, Swarovski, Lladro, Lilliput Lane, Lowell Davis, Wee Forest Folk, David Winter, M.I. Hummel.

- **Secondary Market Terms:** Collectors' purchase of any retired or secondary market item is quality-assured. Daily shipments via UPS. No consignments. Call or write with prices of any items for sale.

- **Business History:** Swan Galleries has a respected history of involvement in secondary and retired figurines, expanding its expertise in Lowell Davis to further involvement in Department 56, Lilliput Lane, Lladro and other collectibles as listed. Swan Galleries is family-owned and operated and is a full-service collectible center for the popular lines. The firm is an active member of the National Association of Limited Edition Dealers (NALED).

• • • • • • •

Swan Seekers Network

4118 East Vernon Avenue
Phoenix, AZ 85008
Phone: 602/957-6294
Fax: 602/957-6294

- **Store Hours:** Monday–Friday: 7:00-8:30 am, Monday–Friday: 12:00 noon-8:00, Saturday and Sunday: 10:00-6:00.

- **Secondary Market Lines:** Swarovski.

- **Secondary Market Terms:** Swan Seekers Network is an information service designed to put sellers and buyers of Swarovski Silver Crystal in direct contact with each other. Buyer and seller registration fees are registrants' choice of $15 up front or 10% at time of transaction. Swan Seekers Network will send you complete information.

- **Business History:** Maret Webb AIA, registered Architect and managing partner of Vehr/Webb Studio, has been collecting Swarovski Silver Crystal since 1978. In 1989, Maret established Swan Seekers Network as a system whereby buyers and sellers of Swarovski Silver Crystal could find each other. Swan Seekers Network is devoted strictly to the Swarovski secondary market. Swan Seekers Network participants include Swarovski collectors in the United States and 15 foreign countries, as well as retailers, insurance companies and estate executors.

"Swan Seekers News" is published three times annually. It includes articles on Swarovski connoisseurship, features on Swarovski collectors, answers to collectors' questions and a secondary market report. Subscription fee is $15.00 per year in US and $22.50 per year for foreign address. Sample issue available for $5.00.

The Thorpe House Country Inn

Clayborne Street
Metamora, IN 47030
Phone: 317/647-5425
Phone: 317/932-2365

- **Store Hours:** Daily, except Monday: 10:00-5:00. Phone orders - Daily: 9:00-9:00.

- **Secondary Market Lines:** Cat's Meow.

- **Secondary Market Terms:** Some consignments. Buy outright. Call for details.

- **Business History:** There aren't many places where collectors can enjoy a leisurely overnight at a charming bed and breakfast, followed by shopping at 100 craft stores. This is all possible, however, in Metamora, Indiana.

  In 1985, Mike and Jean Owens purchased The Thorpe House, an old canaltown home built in 1840. The couple restored this lovely home and transformed it into a bed and breakfast, complete with country cooking and unique gift shops on the premises. The Thorpe House gift shop includes one of the largest selections of Cat's Meow in Southern Indiana. The shop is a Redemption Center for Cat's Meow and features several exclusive custom designed pieces. The Owens have been active in the secondary market since 1988, having several hundred pieces in stock dating back to 1986. They maintain an extensive file on all customers and use this file to match buyers and sellers.

• • • • • • •

Timeless Gifts & Collectibles

5000 E. Market St.
Warren, OH 44484
Phone: 216/856-7886

- **Store Hours:** Monday–Saturday: 10:00-8:00. Sunday: 12:00-4:00.

- **Secondary Market Lines:** Tom Clark Gnomes, All God's Children, Precious Moments, Sarah's Attic, Department 56: Snowbabies, Legends, Raikes Bears, Duncan Royale.

- **Secondary Market Terms:** Consignments. Buy out-right. Match buyers and sellers. Call for details.

- **Business History:** Tony and Pam Limperos always enjoyed collecting, which they did as they traveled with their family. With their family grown and Pam looking at different job opportunities, it seemed like a natural to enter the retail field and sell collectibles. There was room in the area for another collectibles store, so in 1990, Timeless Gifts & Collectibles opened its doors in their present 3,700 square foot facility.

  Today, the store carries a full line of gifts and collectibles, in addition to cards and novelty gifts. Each collectible line carried is stocked extensively. In addition to the lines above, they feature United Design, Dynasty, Middleton, Nahrgang, Emmett Kelly, Jr., Windstone, Memories of Yesterday, Lilliput Lane and North American Bears. Tony and Pam also host about three annual open houses.

The Tinder Box

412 N.W. Plaza
St. Ann, MO 63074
Phone: 314/298-7134

176 Jamestown Mall
Florissant, MO 63034
Phone: 314/741-0899

- **Store Hours:** Monday–Saturday: 10:00-9:30. Sunday: 12:00-6:00.

- **Secondary Market Lines:** M.I. Hummel, Chilmark, Emmett Kelly, Jr., David Winter, Norman Rockwell, Krystonia, Memories of Yesterday, Anheuser-Busch steins.

- **Secondary Market Terms:** Consignments. Buy outright. Locator service. Buy/sell brokerage. Contact Larry or Marsha.

- **Business History:** Larry and Marsha McSpadden were in the restaurant business and doing very well, but decided that a career change was in order. The owner of the Jamestown Tinder Box was moving to California, and this seemed like the perfect opportunity for the McSpaddens. Larry, a pipe collector, understood the inner workings of the collectibles field and changed the Tinder Box's thrust from that of novelties and gifts, to a concentration of collectibles. The couple went on to open up a second store in St. Ann. Today, their knowledgeable staff is thoroughly trained and knows all lines carried, in order to offer optimum assistance to collectors. The stores are Redemption Centers for the lines listed above and host artist appearances about three times annually.

Tower Jewelers

270 Main St.
Hackensack, NJ 07601
Phone: 201/487-9092

- **Store Hours:** Monday–Saturday: 9:45-5:15.

- **Secondary Market Lines:** Swarovski, including candleholders, paperweights; Silver Deer.

- **Secondary Market Terms:** Buy/sell brokerage. Buy outright, consignment. Call for details.

- **Business History:** Tower Jewelers has been family owned and operated by three generations since 1947. Owner Gary Bleiweiss runs a service oriented business. As a jewelry store, the firm is very quality conscious, and this philosophy carries over to the collectibles area as well.

  Tower Jewelers is a Redemption Center for Swarovski and Silver Deer. Their knowledgeable staff maintains contact with its collectible customers by sending postcards announcing the availability of crystal pieces and advance notice on retired items.

Treasure Chest Gift Shop

1221 E. Powell Blvd.
Gresham, OR 97030
Phone: 503/667-2999
Phone: 800/228-1297

- **Store Hours:** Tuesday–Friday: 10:00-5:00. Saturday: 10:00-2:00.

- **Secondary Market Lines:** David Winter, Lilliput Lane, Royal Doulton, Precious Moments, Maud Humphrey, Memories of Yesterday, M.I. Hummel, all collector plates.

- **Secondary Market Terms:** Consignments. Buy outright. Some trade. Layaways available.

- **Business History:** Avid collectors for over twenty years, Jean and Wayne Chapman decided to turn their hobby into a business in 1987, when they opened the Treasure Chest Gift Shop. The store is a Redemption Center for the lines listed above, all of which have collector clubs. They are also a Bradford dealer and a member of NALED. Jean and Wayne pride themselves on their personalized service, with satisfaction guaranteed to each and every collector. The couple enjoys helping collectors locate retired pieces, where often times, the search requires six months to a year before the item is located.

• • • • • • •

Troy Stamp & Coin
Gifts & Collectibles

3275 Rochester Road
Troy, MI 48083
Phone: 313/528-1181
Phone: 800/522-8769
Fax: 313/528-1565

- **Store Hours:** Monday-Friday: 10:00-8:00. Saturday: 10:00-5:00. Sunday: 12:00-5:00.

- **Secondary Market Lines:** Bradford Exchange plates, Hamilton plates, Ashton-Drake dolls, Gorham dolls, Kaiser dolls, Marty Bell, Thomas Kindade, Edna Hibel, Donald Zolan, Sandra Kuck, Masseria, Terry Redlin, Precious Moments, Irish Dresden, M.I. Hummel, Department 56: all villages and accessories, Snowbabies, snowglobes, plates; David Winter, Lilliput Lane, Malcolm Cooper, Tom Clark, Emmett Kelly Jr., Krystonia, Enchantica, Legends, Randy Puckett Whales, Chilmark, Duncan Royale,Whitley Bay Santas, Goebel Miniatures, Sarah's Attic, Lowell Davis, ANRI, Enesco Treasury ornaments, Salvino, Gartlan, Sports Impressions.

- **Secondary Market Terms:** Buy outright. If item isn't in stock, they will try to locate for collector. Satisfaction guaranteed.

- **Business History:** Collectors may be fooled by this store's name, but, in fact, this firm carries more than 60 lines of figurines and is a Redemption Center for more than twenty collector clubs! Owners Tom and Alexa England have been in business since 1981. The firm offers a 60-day layaway plan, appraisal services, a place on their preferred mailing list, and several incentive plans. Call for details.

Tudor Rose Tearoom

480 Liberty
Salem, OR 97301
Phone: 503/588-2345

THE TUDOR
ROSE TEAROOM

- **Store Hours:** Monday-Friday: 9:00-5:30. Saturday: 12:00-5:00.
  (Extended holiday hours: Open Sundays in December - 12:00-5:00.)

- **Secondary Market Lines:** Lilliput Lane, David Winter,
  Lladro, M.I. Hummel, Thomas Kinkade, Britain's Soldiers
  (metal soldiers).

- **Secondary Market Terms:** Buy/sell brokerage.

- **Business History:** Since 1984, Mrs. Joy V. Jones has
  owned and operated the Tudor Rose Tearoom. It should
  come as no surprise that she is originally from England and
  shares part of her heritage with collectors who visit this lovely store.

  The Tudor Rose Tearoom is a Redemption Center for Lilliput
  Lane, David Winter, Lladro, M.I. Hummel, and Thomas
  Kinkade. Mrs. Jones arranges for artist appearances
  throughout the year and offers an appraisal service. She is
  particularly knowlegeable about the David Winter and
  Lilliput Lane lines, which is appropriate, given her background.

  What makes this business unique is its authentic tearoom,
  which serves breakfast, luncheon and high tea daily.

The Village Exchange

P.O. Box 6135
Louisville, KY 40206

- **Hours:** By mail only.

- **Secondary Market Lines:** Department 56.

- **Secondary Market Terms:** Buy Sell Trade ads. No commission charged.

- **Business History:** After 25 years in the giftware and collectible industry, Jack Skeels founded "The Village Exchange" newsletter, in response to Department 56 collector demands for information about retired and limited pieces. "The Village Exchange" is an attractive quarterly newsletter available through selected Department 56 retail shops and by yearly subscription for $20.00 a year. All issues feature the popular buy-sell-trade ads, using a unique system to match buyers and sellers. Collectors who purchase "The Village Exchange" are immediately members of a network of collectors who are seeking Department 56 pieces. The reader uses a certificate which comes in each newsletter to place a free ad or answer up to three ads. Collectors answer the ads by placing the required information on notecards. "The Village Exchange" staff then sorts the cards and refers collectors to the person who placed the ad. Phone numbers and addresses are never printed in the ads; instead, each ad is assigned a private box number. The privacy of this system is its hallmark. Each issue has news about clubs and collector related events and a "Prices From The Marketplace" section listing a high and low price range for all retired and limited Department 56 lighted houses. Except for the newsletter cost, there are no fees or commissions for buyer or seller.

Village Peddler

4275 Harrison Avenue
Cincinnati, OH 45211
Phone: 513/574-8886

- **Store Hours:** Tuesday-Saturday: 10:00-4:30.

- **Secondary Market Lines:** Cat's Meow.

- **Secondary Market Terms:** Will buy outright or trade for retired Cat's Meow.

- **Business History:** The Village Peddler opened in November, 1990 to ring in that year's Yuletide season. Owners Ron and Joan Sanderson renovated a charming two-story 55-year-old building, which presently houses Christmas year round, in addition to carrying Sandicast and United Design animal figurines, Rowe pottery, dollhouses and miniatures, and a very large collection of retired Cat's Meow houses and accessories. A special Christmas atmosphere abounds, with fourteen to sixteen decorated trees and numerous Santas and nutcrackers in stock.

• • • • • • •

Village Plate Collector

120 Forrest Avenue
Cocoa, FL 32922
Phone: 800/PLATES-1
Phone: 407/636-6914

The Village Plate Collector
*The Finest in Limited Edition Collectables
and Fine Furniture*

Charter Member N.A.L.E.D.

- **Store Hours:** Monday–Saturday: 10:00-6:00. Extended holiday hours include Sunday and evening hours. Call for details.

- **Secondary Market Lines:** Bradford, Hibel, Lladro, Department 56, M.I. Hummel, Olszewski Miniatures, Legends, Swarovski, Memories of Yesterday, Armani, Caithness paperweights.

- **Secondary Market Terms:** Buy outright. Match buyers and sellers.

- **Business History:** The Village Plate Collector is one of the finest collectibles stores in central Florida. A charter member of NALED, Lois Felder has owned and operated the store since 1975. A Redemption Center for M.I. Hummel, Swarovski, Armani, Lladro, Memories of Yesterday, Legends and Caithness, The Village Plate Collector is also an Authorized Dealer for Department 56 and a Preferred Dealer for Legends. Several in-store promotions, with noted collectibles artists, are held throughout the year.

  The Village Plate Collector has been selected as a Silver Crystal Award winner in the 1992 GIFT & DECORATIVE ACCESSORIES Award Competition, receiving the Award for outstanding achievement in Gift and Decorative Accessories Shop Design. Lois Felder has been active in the secondary market since 1975, and, The Village Plate Collector is a complete resource center for retired limited edition plates.

• • • • • • •

The Village Press™

1625 Myott Avenue
Rockford, IL 61103-6284
Phone: 815/965-0901

- **Office Hours:** Daily: 8:00-5:00. After hours and weekends: if they are in, they will answer.

- **Secondary Market Lines:** Department 56: Snow Village, Heritage Village, Snowbabies, Department 56 ornaments.

- **Secondary Market Terms:** 20% brokerage fee. Seller pays fee. Sales guaranteed. Retired Department 56 ornaments, buying outright. No charge cards, personal checks require 10 days to clear. Newsletter subscription, $20 (US), ($23 US to all other countries) for eight issues. Free sample copy.

- **Business History:** "The Village Press"™ is an independent, secondary market newsletter for Department 56 collectors. Published eight times per year, the newsletter offers news and views about the Original Snow Village Collection, the Heritage Village Collections and Snowbabies. Feature articles cover "Sightings," what to look for in new introductions, what's hot on the secondary market, as well as exclusive articles on related items. The first independent newsletter for Department 56 collectors, the premier issue mailed in April 1988 to fifteen collectors. Readership now is over 5,000! They also offer a brokerage service for retired designs, issue secondary market price guides, and provide assistance in settling insurance claims. "The Village Press"™ is not affiliated with Department 56.

Villages Classified

P.O. Box 34166
Granada Hills, CA 91394
Phone: 818/368-6765

- **Office Hours:** Monday–Friday: 9:00-7:00.

- **Secondary Market Lines:** All Department 56 and collectible villages.

- **Secondary Market Terms:** Publication: buyers and sellers are matched through the ads they place in this publication.

- **Business History:** The "Villages Classified" is a unique advertising media printed exclusively for Department 56 collectors. Collectors can now find other collectors to buy, sell and trade Department 56 pieces nationwide in the secondary market via "Villages Classified." There is no commission involved -- only the cost of a subscription.

  Paul and Mirta Burns are the editor/owners of the "Villages Classified." Mirta draws upon her twelve years of experience as an active collector and secondary market trader to bring collectors together in the Burns' "Villages Classified." Collectors who subscribe to this informative monthly publication receive a free 30-word listing. "Villages Classified" also accepts ads from non-subscribers. The closing date is the 15th of each month.

• • • • • • •

Von Reece & Daughters Christmas Keepsakes

4400 Bunny Run
Austin, TX 78746
Phone: 512/327-6800
Phone: 800/346-7575
Fax: 512/327-5524

- **Office Hours:** Monday–Friday: 10:00-5:00.

- **Secondary Market Lines:** Hallmark: Keepsake ornaments and miniatures, Little Gallery ornaments and pendants; Enesco: Treasury ornaments (Premier Dealer), musical figurines, (Enesco Musical Showcase Dealer), Memories of Yesterday figurines and ornaments, North Pole Village, and Brambly Hedge.

- **Secondary Market Terms:** Consignment. Buy outright. Call for details. Layaway also available.

- **Business History:** Von Reece & Daughters Christmas Keepsakes is a family-owned business, with husband Von, wife Connie Sr., and daughters Laurie and Connie Jr. actively involved in this collectibles firm. Since 1975, Von Reece & Daughters has been active in the Collector Car Auction business; this division was sold in December of 1991. The Christmas Keepsakes division was started in December of 1990. Today, the firm is mainly a mail order business, carrying a full line of Enesco Treasury ornaments on the primary market. Collectors may also purchase retired Hallmark and Enesco pieces. Closer to Christmas, the firm rents a storefront in the mall. Call for store location. Collectors may write or call toll free for a quarterly price list.

Wayside Country Store

1015 Boston Post Road
Marlboro, MA 01752
Phone: 508/481-3458
Fax: 508/485-4978

- **Store Hours:** Daily: 10:00-5:00.

- **Secondary Market Lines:** Byers' Choice Carolers, Sebastian Miniatures.

- **Secondary Market Terms:** Consignments. No buy outrights. Auction in September of Byers' Choice Carolers.

- **Business History:** Located in an historic building owned formerly by auto magnate, Henry Ford, is the Wayside Country Store in Marlboro, Massachusetts. Tony and Joan Scerra opened their store in 1974, retaining its charm of yesteryear.

  Wayside is the largest single dealer for Byers' Choice fig-urines. Collectors may join this firm's in-store Byers' Choice club for $5.00, which entitles them to a quarterly newsletter, advance notice of availability of pieces and other incentives. Each September, Wayside hosts the popular "Dickens of a Day" featuring various Byers' Choice activities. Collectors can view rare carolers, participate in artist signings and attend an auction of old Carolers.

  Wayside Country Store is a Redemption Center for Precious Moments, Sebastian Miniatures, David Winter, M.I. Hummel, Lilliput Lane, Chilmark Pewter and Jan Hagara. They also carry Department 56, Cat's Meow, Lizzie High, Wee Forest Folk and many others.

Weston's Limited Editions

Monmouth Mall
Eatontown, NJ 07724
Phone: 908/542-3550
Phone: 800/526-2391
Fax: 908/747-6861

- **Store Hours:** Monday–Saturday: 10:00-9:30, Sunday: 12:00-5:00.

- **Secondary Market Lines:** Ashton-Drake, Bradford plates, Department 56: Snowbabies, Dicken's Village, New England, Christmas in the City, Alpine Village, Snow Village; Kurt S. Adler nutcrackers, Armani Club, Byers' Choice, Duncan Royale, Goebel miniatures, David Winter, M.I. Hummel, Lawtons, Lladro, Swarovski, Mattel: Barbie, Timeless Creations; Precious Moments, All God's Children, Memories of Yesterday, Lowell Davis.

- **Secondary Market Terms:** Buy outright. Call for details.

- **Business History:** The largest collectible retailer on the central New Jersey shore, Weston's offers its customers a wide variety of collectibles. Established in 1979 by Art and Hermine Weston, the couple are also principals of Parkwest Publications, Inc., publishing collectibles catalogs, which are distributed by NALED retailers across the country. Recognized by The Bradford Exchange as the Dealer of the Year in 1990, Weston's also runs a doll mail order business. They send informative doll newsletters to their customers, informing them about current releases. Weston's also hosts ten to twelve artist appearances throughout the year.

What The Dickens

2885 W. Ribera Place
Tucson, AZ 85741
Phone: 602/297-7019

- **Store Hours:** Monday-Saturday: 9:00-9:00.

- **Secondary Market Lines:** Department 56: Snow
Village, Dickens Village, Christmas in the City, New England
Village, Alpine Village, North Pole, Snowbabies, Winter
Silhouette.

- **Secondary Market Terms:** No consignments. A buy-
sell/trade publication offering subscriptions. 10% commission charged to the buyer, 10% commission on trades split
between traders. Call for details.

- **Business History:** What the Dickens has been a secondary market broker since November, 1991. Owners
Kenneth and Judith Isaacson have been collectors of Dickens
Village and Snowbabies since 1990. They publish a bi-
monthly secondary market publication offered to collectors
for $15.00 per year. All sales are handled personally, and
items are shipped UPS insured. Besides offering a money
back guarantee, What the Dickens appraises Department 56
pieces for collectors.

• • • • • • •

The Windsor Shoppe

117 Washington Ave.
North Haven, CT 06473
Phone: 203/239-4644 - ask for Chris
Fax: 203/234-1882

- **Store Hours:** Monday–Wednesday: 10:00-6:00. Thursday-Friday: 10:00-9:00. Saturday: 9:30-6:00. Extended hours between Thanksgiving and Christmas.

- **Secondary Market Lines:** Department 56, Precious Moments.

- **Secondary Market Terms:** Buy/Sell brokerage. No commission is charged. Seller is asked to make a donation to his/her favorite charity.

- **Business History:** Gary Benzel's father Mort started a card shop in 1968, which also carried a small selection of gift items. It wasn't until a customer walked into the store one day requesting a $50 anniversary gift, that they looked into carrying collectibles. The store first featured Hummels and then Lladros. Gary then continued stocking the store, until he carried every major collectible line. Today, the store is a Redemption Center for every major collector club and one of the largest collectible stores in Connecticut at 10,000 square feet.

  The Windsor Shoppe is committed to educating its customers to make them more knowledgeable about their hobby. The store hosts at least twelve open houses and artist appearances annually. Customers are also mailed a quarterly newsletter, "Focus on Collectibles." The Windsor Shoppe is a member of both NALED and Gift Creations Concepts.

The Wishing Well

444 Alisal Rd.
Solvang, CA 93463
Phone: 805/688-6261

- **Store Hours:** Daily: 9:00-5:00.

- **Secondary Market Lines:** David Winter, Gartlan USA, Jan Hagara, ANRI (Disney only), Ron Lee.

- **Secondary Market Terms:** Buy-sell brokerage. 10% commission.

- **Business History:** Located in Solvang, the Danish capital of America, is The Wishing Well, owned by Bob and Marge Phillips. Two million visitors stroll the three-block village annually, enjoying the architecture and experiencing the Danish culture. Tourists flock to Danish Days, which are held the third weekend in September each year. They are treated to Danish dancers in the street, wandering Danish bands, all dressed in native costumes -- and mouth-watering Danish delicacies.

It is here that The Wishing Well has provided top-notch collectibles services for eleven years. Bob Phillips is considered an authority on David Winter cottages. He offers an appraisal service and holds one of the largest David Winter shows in the world. Collectors are delighted by the English artists who autograph and embellish the cottages during this grand affair.

Bob knows the importance of staying in touch with his customers and does so with the use of postcards informing collectors about the availability of collector club exclusives, retired announcements and special events.

• • • • • • •

Wooden Skate Antiques
Estate Jewelry & Gems

1259 West Grand River Avenue
Okemos, MI 48864
Phone: 517/349-1515
Fax: 517/349-8628

- **Store Hours:** Monday–Saturday: 10:00-5:30, except Thursday to 8:00.

- **Secondary Market Lines:** M.I. Hummel, Royal Doulton mugs and plates, Norman Rockwell, Royal Copenhagen, Bing & Grondahl, Mme. Alexander dolls, etc.

- **Secondary Market Terms:** Consignment. Buy outright.

- **Business History:** Opened in 1973, Wooden Skate is one of the oldest and largest antiques establishments in Michigan, with two locations and 35,000 square feet. Owner Gary Durow, who has made buys around the world, writes columns for trade and general publications, is regularly featured on radio call-in shows regarding antiques and collectibles, and offers expert appraisal services. The shop, whose storefront resembles an 1800s village, is so charming that tour buses often stop to allow their passengers to explore the lovely grounds and facilities. Both Wooden Skate stores are featured in the Capitol Area Antiques Trail, which includes 300 dealers within a 20-mile drive.

Worldwide Collectibles and Gifts

P.O. Box 158
2 Lakeside Avenue
Berwyn, PA 19312-0158
Phone: 215/644-2442
Fax: 215/889-9549

- **Store Hours:** Monday–Saturday: 10:00-5:00. Operators on duty 24-hours a day for orders and inquiries.

- **Secondary Market Lines:** Swarovski, Lladro, M.I. Hummel, David Winter, Duncan Royale, Steiff, plates, bells, collector club pieces.

- **Secondary Market Terms:** No consignments. Call for specific quotes. Prompt payment on all items purchased. Prompt delivery on items sold.

- **Business History:** Worldwide Collectibles is a full service company established in 1975, specializing in most major brands of collectibles. Dealing in current and secondary market pieces, Worldwide has particular expertise in full lines of Swarovski, Lladro, M.I. Hummel, David Winter, Duncan Royale, Precious Moments, Steiff, collector plates, bells, and collector club pieces. The company maintains large inventories on all lines carried, with a mail order catalog available.

  Thoroughly experienced in appraisals, references are available upon request. The Worldwide staff is actively involved with major insurers for replacement and estimate valuation purposes.

• • • • • • •

Young's Ltd.

1028 Boardwalk
Ocean City, NJ 08226
Phone: 609/399-9515

Young's Ltd.
FINE GIFTS • FINE JEWELRY • ART OBJECTS

- **Store Hours:** January-June: 10:00-5:00 daily. Closed Tuesdays. July-September: 10:00-11:00 daily. October-December: 10:00-6:00 daily.

- **Secondary Market Lines:** Department 56: All Villages and accessories, Snowbabies; Precious Moments, Krystonia, Tom Clark Gnomes, Lowell Davis, Sarah's Attic, All God's Children, Lladro, Wee Forest Folk, PenniBears, Maud Humphrey, David Winter, Lilliput Lane, Armani, ANRI, Emmett Kelly, Jr., Rockwell, Swarovski, Sports Impressions, M.I. Hummel, and many others.

- **Secondary Market Terms:** Consignments. Some buy outright. Layaways available.

- **Business History:** Even before Arnold and Julia Young established their business in 1974, both had extensive experience in the arts. Arnold had owned an antique store, and Julia's family had sold jewelry and art objects for years. Today, the pair has combined their talents to market the top collectibles lines at Young's. Located in a tourist area, the Youngs realize the importance of providing a large and knowledgeable staff to assist their visiting collector. Young's is enhanced by its ten year affiliation with Gift Creations Concepts. The store also hosts open houses and artist appearances weekly during the summer. The Youngs maintain a secondary market wish list for collectors who are searching for retired pieces.

Zaslow's Fine Collectibles

Strathmore Shopping Center Rt. 34
Matawan, NJ 07747
Phone: 908/583-1499
Fax: 908/583-0748

- **Store Hours:** Monday–Saturday: 10:00-6:00. Fridays until 8:00. Sunday: by appointment. Telephone or fax anytime.

- **Secondary Market Lines:** All plates, including Bradford , Delphi, W.S. George, Hamilton and more!; M.I. Hummel, Krystonia, B.P. Gutmann, Maud Humphrey and other figurines.

- **Secondary Market Terms:** Locator service for old plates and Norman Rockwell figurines. Collectors who wish to sell plates, are invited to submit a list of asking prices. This information is put on file, and plates are purchased as needed.

- **Business History:** Zaslow's Fine Collectibles has been in business since 1975 and offers nearly all active collectible lines. Zaslow's is a charter member of NALED and owner Irv Zaslow was a founding director of that prestigious dealer organization.

  Zaslow's specializes in locating out-of-production collector plates. It can take two days to two years to find a plate, but Irv Zaslow and his staff will pursue every lead possible to locate the collectible requested. Zaslow's hosts ten to twelve open houses annually and sends mailings to its active customers. Appraisals are also available.

Index By Location

Darle's Dolls & Bears
Eve's Collectors' Show
GRAHAM'S CRACKERS and Other
   Collectables
MSdataBase Solutions
Larry Rager's Gifts of Perfecton
Rose Marie's
Shirley's Collectibles—"Hoosier Happening"
The Thorpe House Country Inn

Iowa
The Baggage Car

Kansas
Carol's Cards & Gifts
Gifts & Accents
Lancelot's

Kentucky
Morris Antiques
The Village Exchange

Louisiana
Charity's Gift Shop
Dickens' Exchange, Inc.

Maryland
Bodzer's Collectibles
Cherry Tree Cards & Gifts Inc.
Figurine World
Imagine That!
The Plate Niche

Massachusetts
B.J. Dolls & Gifts
Boston Pewter Co.
Cheerios
Cuties, Bears & Stuffies
The Handmaiden
New England Collectibles Exchange
Osterville Newstand
Stacy's Gifts & Collectibles
Wayside Country Store

Michigan
Brewhaus™ Gift Shop
C-n-A Collectibles
Collectors Unlimited
The Diamond Connection
Georgia's Gift Gallery
House Of Cards Limited
The Mole Hole of Kalamazoo
Robinette's Gift Barn
Troy Stamp & Coin, Gifts & Collectibles
Wooden Skate Antiques Estate Jewelry
   & Gems

Minnesota
Collector's Choice

Collectors Gallery & Landmark Collectors'
   Exchange
Papillon Ltd.
The Steinhaus

Missouri
Collectible House
Jerdón
The Tinder Box

Montana
The Ship's Bell

Nebraska
Collectors Plates

New Hampshire
The Great American Country Store
Quality Collectables

New Jersey
Collectors' Emporium
Jiana Inc.
La Maison Capri, Inc.
Prestige Collections
Tower Jewelers
Weston's Limited Editions
Young's Ltd.
Zaslow's Fine Collectibles

New Mexico
Don's Collectibles

New York
Alisa's Dolls
A Work Of Art
Collectible Finders Service
Collectibly Yours
Eureka! Collectibles
Glorious Treasures
Island Treasures
The Limited Edition
Stephens-A Touch of Christmas Plus

North Carolina
Callahan's Of Calabash
The Gift Attic

Ohio
Buchanan Place
Collectible Exchange, Inc.
Colonial House Antiques
Curio Cabinet & Christmas Village
Gingerbread House Gifts & Collectibles
Great Lakes Gnome Exchange
Miller's Hallmark & Gift Gallery
Rochelle's Fine Gifts
Secondary Collectible Service
Sterling & Collectables Inc.
Story Book Kids

Timeless Gifts & Collectibles
Village Peddler

Oklahoma
Kabet's

Oregon
Lita Sale Import
The Old Miller Place
Treasure Chest Gift Shop
Tudor Rose Tea Room

Pennsylvania
Bob Lamson Beer Steins, Inc.
Carousel Collectibles
Collector's Marketplace
Country Charm House
Crayon Soup
The Emporium
Sam's Steins & Collectibles
Saville's Limited Editions
Worldwide Collectibles & Gifts

Tennessee
Barbara's Gatlinburg Shops
HI Hat Collectibles
The Lemon Tree
Morton's Antique & Estate Jewelry
Our Place — A General Store

Texas
Amanda's Fine Gifts
Collector's Alley
Eloise's Gifts & Antiques
Keepsakes & Kollectibles
OHI Exchange
The Ornament Connection
Serendipity
Spencer's China & Gallery
Village Realty/"The Cottage Collector"
Von Reece & Daughters Christmas
    Keepsakes

Utah
D & A Investments

Vermont
Christmas In Vermont

Virginia
Biggs Limited Editions
Karolson's Treasures
Memories in Motion

Washington
Collectors' Marketplace
FACET Collector's Showcase
Natalia's Collectibles
Sier's Secondary Exchange

Wisconsin
Collectibles etc., Inc.
Cottage Park
Mader's

Canada
Shanfields-Meyers

Index

Gutmann, Bessie Pease, 28, 41, 96, 201

—H—

Hackett-American, 3, 137, 172
Hagara, Jan, 2, 14, 28, 37, 38, 40, 44, 49, 50, 53, 60, 67, 74, 75, 78, 80, 86, 89, 95, 96, 105, 119, 131, 133, 139, 141, 143, 157, 169, 197
Haley, Alex, 60, 113
Hall, Kristi, 1
Hallmark, 6, 8, 9, 26, 32, 37, 40, 42, 49, 72, 80, 92, 105, 112, 134, 135, 138, 145, 168, 169, 192
    Cookie cutters, Hallmark, 9
    Light & Motion, 32
    Little Gallery, 9, 192
    Magnets, 9
    Merry Miniatures, 9, 26, 32, 38, 134
    Pins, 9
    Stocking hangers, 9
    Table decorations, 9
Hamilton Collection, 3, 14, 16, 37, 42, 43, 57, 65, 67, 71, 78, 89, 131, 147, 148, 149, 167, 185, 201
Hamilton Heritage dolls, 42, 90, 149
Hamms, 19, 66, 85, 122, 161, 174
Hand & Hammer, 176
Hap Henricksen's Wizards & Dragons, 108
Hartland, USA, 3, 151
Haviland, 166
Heileman, 66, 161
Heineken, 122
Hibel, Edna, 52, 86, 96, 104, 185, 189
Himstedt, Annette, 1, 36, 43, 65, 67, 94, 128, 157
Hine, John, 37, 88
Hook, Francis, 96
Houses, see Cottages
Hudson Pewter, 11, 108, 148
Hudson Village, 98
Hummel, M.I., 2, 4, 6, 16, 25, 28, 29, 30, 31, 36, 37, 38, 40, 41, 42, 43, 47, 48, 49, 50, 51, 53, 54, 55, 62, 70, 71, 74, 76, 77, 78, 79, 82, 83, 84, 86, 91, 92, 96, 104, 105, 106, 109, 111, 114, 121, 123, 125, 126, 127, 129, 130, 133, 135, 142, 143, 144, 148, 150, 156, 157, 158, 159, 160, 162, 163, 165, 166, 167, 169, 170, 173, 178, 182, 184, 185, 186, 189, 194, 198, 199, 200, 201
Hummel, Century, 77
Humphrey, Maud, 2, 6, 11, 12, 14, 16, 21, 28, 35, 36, 37, 39, 44, 49, 50, 52, 53, 57, 60, 62, 64, 65, 67, 74, 78, 80, 89, 96, 105, 106, 110, 120, 132, 133, 135, 139, 141, 143, 147, 155, 157, 162, 177, 184, 200, 201
Hutschenreuther, 166

—I—

Incolay, 44
International, 176
Iris Arc, 136
Irish Dresden, 185
Ispanky, 37, 166

—J—

Jem dolls, 8
John Hine, see Hine, John

—K—

Kaiser, 78, 148, 166, 185
Kelly, Emmett Jr., 28, 29, 35, 37, 52, 62, 74, 78, 80, 84, 89, 96, 109, 110, 111, 121, 123, 125, 132, 139, 143, 148, 162, 163, 169, 177, 182, 185, 200; see also Flambro
Kinkade, Thomas, 53, 110, 116, 141, 157, 159, 171, 185, 186
Kirk-Stieff, 55, 176
Knot Knoggins, 175
Krystonia, 6, 11, 16, 22, 38, 39, 52, 75, 78, 84, 104, 118, 129, 136, 143, 169, 170, 175, 182, 185, 200, 201
Kuck, Sandra, 41, 42, 44, 67, 78, 90, 96, 114, 142, 157, 185

—L—

Ladie & Friends, 78, 98
Lalique, 150, 158, 165, 166
Land of Legend, 108
Laura's Attic, 23
Lawrence, Christopher, 88
Lawtons, 94, 194
Layton, Corinne, 114
Lee, Ron, 4, 75, 82, 83, 110, 113, 121, 124, 139, 158, 197
Lefton, 6, 37
Legends, 5, 12, 16, 17, 36, 37, 53, 57, 73, 78, 83, 103, 104, 109, 110, 115, 129, 154, 171, 175, 181, 185, 189
Lenox, 78, 159
Lexington Hall, 148
Lilliput Lane, 6, 10, 11, 12, 14, 22, 24, 29, 31, 33, 35, 36, 37, 38, 39, 40, 44, 48, 49, 50, 51, 52, 53, 54, 56, 57, 59, 62, 64, 73, 77, 78, 82, 83, 84, 91, 92, 95, 98, 101, 105, 106, 108, 109, 110, 111, 113, 118, 123, 125, 129, 132, 143, 148, 154, 160, 162,

Whitley Bay, 6, 52, 78, 185
Wideman, Maurice, 54, 78, 88, 100, 129,
    135, 142
Wieghorst, Olaf, 129
Wildlife, 108
Windy Meadows, 12, 74
Winter, David, 6, 8, 11, 12, 13, 14, 16, 28,
    29, 31, 33, 34, 35, 36, 37, 38, 39, 40, 44,
    46, 48, 49, 50, 52, 53, 54, 56, 57, 59, 62,
    64, 73, 74, 76, 77, 78, 79, 80, 80, 82, 84,
    88, 89, 91, 92, 95, 101, 103, 104, 105, 106,
    108, 109, 110, 111, 114, 118, 123, 125,
    129, 132, 135, 136, 142, 143, 148, 150,
    154, 155, 157, 158, 159, 160, 162, 163,
    165, 169, 170, 171, 173, 178, 182, 184,
    185, 186, 194, 197, 199, 200
Winter, David, Christmas ornaments, 134
Winton-Roland, 167
Wolfe, Tim, 100, 142
World Doll, 3
Woods, Robin, 43, 67
W.S. George, *see* George, W.S.
Wysocki, Charles, 37

—Y—
Yuengling, 161

—Z—
Zolan, Donald, 41, 44, 76, 96, 114, 129, 143,
    157, 159, 185